SYLLOGE OF COINS
OF THE BRITISH ISLES

SYLLOGE OF COINS
OF THE BRITISH ISLES

Published by the British Academy, except No. 8 which is published by the Trustees of the British Museum
All quarto, cloth bound

IN PREPARATION

SYLLOGE OF COINS OF THE BRITISH ISLES

13
ROYAL COLLECTION OF COINS AND MEDALS NATIONAL MUSEUM COPENHAGEN

PART III A

Anglo-Saxon Coins: Cnut
mints Axbridge–Lymne

BY

GEORG GALSTER

*Fil. Dr., Formerly Keeper of the Royal Collection of
Coins and Medals*

No. 1032

LONDON
PUBLISHED FOR THE BRITISH ACADEMY
AND THE CARLSBERG FOUNDATION
by the OXFORD UNIVERSITY PRESS, LONDON, W. I
and SPINK & SON LIMITED
5–7 KING STREET, ST. JAMES'S, LONDON, S. W. I
1970

PRINTED IN GREAT BRITAIN
AT THE UNIVERSITY PRESS, OXFORD
BY VIVIAN RIDLER
PRINTER TO THE UNIVERSITY

CONTENTS

vi CONTENTS

FOREWORD

On behalf of the Royal Collection of Coins and Medals in Copenhagen it is my pleasant duty to express my sincere thanks to all who have helped towards the publication of parts IIIA, IIIB, and IIIc of our *Sylloge of Coins of the British Isles*. In Denmark the Rask-Ørsted Fond and Statens almindelige Videnskabsfond have again made important grants for salaries and for photography, while the Carlsberg Fond has undertaken to cover half of the costs of printing in addition to a personal grant for Dr. Georg Galster, which has enabled him to continue his work. This, however, has been made much easier by the invaluable assistance of Lars Haastrup, Esq.

Special thanks are due to the English Sylloge Committee for smooth co-operation and to Messrs. C. E. Blunt and M. Dolley for their competent and efficient work in arranging the manuscript for printing, compiling the indexes, and assisting in the proof-reading.

OTTO MØRKHOLM
Keeper of Coins

EDITORS' NOTE

THE British Academy is once again deeply indebted to Dr. Georg Galster for preparing the following catalogue of the English coins of Cnut in the Royal Danish Collection at Copenhagen.

In this series the collection can be said to rival the Royal Collection at Stockholm and it will be seen that there is an exceptionally large number of moneyers who are not recorded on coins of Cnut for the type by Hildebrand in his catalogue of the Stockholm collection.[1] The six coins from the extremely rare mint of Langport (nos. 1292–7) compare, for instance, with no more than two listed by Hildebrand, one of which is a fragment. The coins of Bridport (nos. 118–19 and 4236) supply, moreover, two types for this mint not found in Hildebrand's catalogue.

As in the volume devoted to the coins of Æthelred II in the Copenhagen collection, the coins have been listed in the order in which they lie in the trays, an arrangement which follows, broadly, that laid down by Hildebrand.

Recent study suggests that a few coins in the catalogue, though superficially part of Cnut's English coinage, are in fact irregular.[2] There is no record of any specimen of the group to which they belong having been found in the British Isles and it seems likely that they were struck in Scandinavia. The coins in question are numbers 50–1, 156, 293, 557, 706, 918, 1486, 1488, 1672–3, 1712, 2148(?), 2156, 2160–1, 2202–5, 2297, 2382–3, 2887, 2944, 2946–50, 3098–3100A, 3136, 3150–3, 3212, 3232, 3318, 3372–3, 3521, 3800, 3842, 3880(?), 4227–34, 4237–4413. At the end of the catalogue, on pls. 152–8, will be found the coins which are palpably imitations of English money. This is the first time that so large an illustrated record of these irregular pieces has been published.

Students in these islands in general regard Hildebrand's types A–D of Cnut as Scandinavian and his types K, I, and F as in fact posthumous.[2] Where a moneyer of one of these types is noted as not being recorded by Hildebrand for the reign, this should, however, be understood as meaning not recorded by him on a coin in the name of Cnut.

The British Academy acknowledges with gratitude the support it has received from the Carlsberg Foundation in the publication of what is the largest illustrated corpus hitherto produced of the coinage in the name

---

[1] *Anglosachsiska Mynt i Svenska Kongliga Myntkabinettet*, by Bror Emil Hildebrand, Stockholm, 1881.

[2] *British Numismatic Journal*, xxx, ii (1961), pp. 235–51.

of Cnut. It is hoped that this will prove of as much interest to numismatists and historians in Denmark as to those in the British Isles.

A final volume will bring the record of this great collection down to 1154.

C.E.B.
M.D.

DONORS, SALES, FINDS, ETC.

THE following is a list of abbreviations used in the catalogue that follows for references to donors, sales, finds, etc. The numbers are those of the pieces in the catalogue from the respective sources.

B.P.; Bytte-protokol. Exchange. F.P.; Fund-protokol. Find.
G.P.; Gave-protokol. Donation. K.P.; Købe-protokol. Purchase.

Aarhus
: 1890. Historisk-antikvarisk Selskab (Historical-antiquarian Society). (B.P. 1267): 298.

Agerskov
: 1922. Carl Christian Agerskov (1853–1923), savings-bank manager in Roskilde. His collection was sold by auction in the Numismatic Society, Copenhagen. See *NFM* vi, no. 24, April–May 1923, pp. 257–70. Several of his coins were found in Roskilde. (G.P. 1732). 318, 2243, 2498.

Ahlander
: 1851. See Part II, p. ix (G.P. 233, 236, 269): 441, 3449, 3476, 4086. The coins were most likely found in Gotland.

Alberts
: Claes Alberts (1767–1840), clerk in the National bank, Copenhagen: 1700.

Appeldorn
: 1867. Frederik Christian Appeldorn (1795–1881), rector in Gørlev-Bakkendrup, Løve herred, Holbæk amt. (G.P. 579): 3561.

Bahrfeldt
: Bahrfeldt, Emil (1850–1929), German numismatist. See Lupow find.

Bech
: 1906. Frederik Christian Bech (1817–1905), judge in Slagelse. Auction 25 April and 10 December 1906 and 29 May 1907. See also *NFM* iii, no. 7, June 1919, pp. 89 f. Several of his coins were most likely found in Slagelse and neighbourhood. (K.P. 1117): 27, 142, 171, 339, 426, 485, 554, 706, 870, 1002, 1034, 1095, 1885, 2300, 2324, 2334, 2341, 2504, 2722, 2863, 2884, 3106, 3112, 3139, 3212, 3226, 3447, 3478, 3539, 3549, 3707, 3808, 3837, 3858–9, 3941, 4008, 4162, 4233, 4256.

Begtrup
: 1857. See Part II, p. ix. (B.P. 407): 1869, 2850.

Benzon
: 1885. Alfred Nicolai Benzon (1823–84), chemist (Svane-pharmacy in Copenhagen from 1849). Auction 6 November 1885–30 April 1888. The donation is printed as an appendix to the sale-catalogue. See Part I, p. 12. (G.P. 982): 145, 194, 235, 394, 456, 543, 574, 625, 680, 688, 766, 936, 943, 977, 1066, 1114, 1145, 1168, 1173, 1304, 1435, 1530, 1572, 1792, 1820, 1939, 2024, 2088, 2107, 2147, 2476, 2570, 2652, 2725, 2771, 3037, 3206, 3260, 3324, 3433, 3502, 3604, 3693, 3723, 3746, 3794, 3886, 3968, 4174.

Bergsøe
: 1877. See Part I, pp. 18 and 43, and Part II, p. ix. See *NFM* iii, no. 7, June 1919, p. 81, *NNÅ* 1949, pp. 10 ff., *NNUM* 1961, pp. 61–7. (K.P. 583): 311, 3880.

Beskrivelse
: 1791. See Part I, pp. 8–9: 59, 117, 293, 579, 650, 665, 714, 756, 1063, 1139, 1330, 1422, 1445, 1834, 1952, 2083, 2120, 2550, 2610, 2685, 2766, 2813, 2994, 3116, 3248, 3510, 3917, 4122, 4137.

3592, 3668, 3708, 3780, 3844, 3914, 3978, 3993, 4031, 4082, 4089, 4153, 4184, 4318, 4359, 4393–4.

Brasch *See* Flensborg.

Bruun 1920. See Part I, pp. 13 and 43. (B.P. 1589): 3019.

Bruun *L. E. Bruuns Mønt- og Medaillesamling* (København 1928): 8, 11–2, 14, 18, 22, 24, 29, 31, 35, 43, 45–7, 51, 58, 60, 62, 64, 70, 78–9, 82–7, 91, 93, 100, 102, 107, 109–10, 114, 121, 129, 131, 134, 136, 146, 149, 154, 156, 160, 162, 166–7, 169, 173, 179, 182, 189, 193, 196, 209, 214, 217, 220, 222, 226–7, 229, 232, 237, 241, 244, 246, 250, 255, 259, 261, 263, 268, 271, 276, 278, 283, 285, 289, 296, 301, 304, 307, 309, 314, 319–20, 325, 332–3, 335, 337, 344, 350, 355, 360, 363, 369, 373, 377, 382–3, 392, 396, 399, 403, 407, 411, 413, 415, 417–18, 421, 424, 427, 433, 435, 437, 439, 444, 448, 450, 454, 465, 475, 481–2, 494, 497, 503, 506, 509, 514, 520, 523, 525–6, 535–6, 539, 541, 545, 547, 549, 553, 557, 561, 569, 576, 581, 594, 596, 599, 600, 608, 611, 615, 617, 624, 631, 636, 638, 643, 645, 656, 662–3, 666, 670, 673, 676, 682, 687, 692, 702, 708–9, 715, 722, 729, 731, 733–4, 736, 738, 741–2, 747, 753, 761, 768, 771, 776, 780, 784, 788, 790, 792, 796, 801, 804, 807, 815, 817, 821, 825, 828–30, 834, 836, 838, 840, 846, 849, 851, 853, 856, 862, 865, 871, 875, 879, 882, 886, 894, 900, 909–10, 912, 915, 920, 923, 925, 930, 933, 945, 950, 952, 954, 957, 959, 966, 969, 974, 980, 981–2, 986, 991, 995–8, 1005, 1008, 1015, 1020, 1022, 1024, 1028, 1030, 1032, 1035, 1037, 1040, 1053, 1056, 1061, 1065, 1073, 1083, 1085, 1089, 1093, 1101, 1104, 1121–2, 1125, 1127, 1130, 1132, 1135, 1137, 1146, 1150, 1152, 1156, 1159–60, 1164, 1169, 1176, 1179, 1182, 1185, 1190, 1197, 1199, 1201, 1211, 1213, 1215, 1219, 1221, 1223, 1225, 1230, 1233, 1239, 1243, 1249, 1253–4, 1261, 1263, 1265, 1270, 1274, 1277, 1285, 1290, 1291, 1296, 1308, 1310, 1313, 1315, 1317, 1319, 1324, 1329, 1331, 1341, 1343, 1350, 1353, 1364, 1367, 1370, 1374, 1376, 1380, 1383, 1389, 1395, 1402, 1410, 1415, 1419, 1421, 1424, 1425, 1426, 1428, 1430–1, 1437, 1439, 1441, 1443, 1451, 1455, 1460, 1468, 1475, 1478, 1483, 1486, 1494, 1498, 1500, 1502, 1504, 1510, 1514, 1518, 1520, 1532, 1534, 1537, 1547, 1552–3, 1555, 1563, 1567, 1570, 1573, 1576, 1582, 1584, 1589, 1592, 1597, 1599, 1601, 1604, 1613, 1620, 1622, 1627, 1629, 1635, 1638, 1640–1, 1647, 1649, 1654, 1657, 1669, 1671–2, 1674, 1680, 1685, 1695, 1700, 1702, 1709, 1712, 1715, 1717, 1721, 1725–6, 1736, 1738, 1742–3, 1748–9, 1754, 1756, 1759, 1765, 1772, 1774, 1777, 1782, 1785–6, 1791, 1794, 1800, 1806, 1809, 1813, 1818, 1822, 1825, 1829, 1838, 1841, 1846, 1849, 1854, 1863, 1865, 1870, 1874, 1878–9, 1891, 1893, 1895, 1898, 1900, 1905, 1912, 1917, 1922, 1924, 1926, 1932, 1934, 1942, 1947, 1953, 1958–9, 1964, 1973, 1977, 1983, 1991, 1994, 1997, 1999, 2001, 2003, 2010, 2014–15, 2019, 2025, 2027, 2031, 2037–8, 2041, 2050, 2057, 2063, 2065, 2067, 2078, 2085, 2086, 2089, 2091, 2095, 2106, 2113, 2117, 2122–3, 2126, 2130, 2136, 2140, 2148, 2151, 2159, 2161, 2163–4, 2167, 2175, 2179, 2182, 2187, 2190, 2192, 2196, 2198, 2201, 2203, 2205, 2209, 2216, 2218, 2221, 2231, 2234, 2237, 2239, 2245, 2247–8,

2259–60, 2263–5, 2268, 2275, 2280–1, 2290, 2293, 2305, 2308,
2312, 2314, 2318, 2328–9, 2338, 2343, 2345, 2352, 2359, 2361,
2364, 2373, 2375, 2381, 2385, 2394, 2396, 2405–6, 2410, 2412,
2415, 2417, 2424, 2433, 2436, 2439–40, 2454, 2456, 2458,
2468, 2474, 2478, 2482, 2486, 2492, 2500, 2510, 2515, 2522, 2525,
2531, 2535, 2543, 2549, 2554, 2559, 2569, 2574, 2576, 2585, 2587,
2591, 2601, 2604, 2606, 2608, 2614, 2617–18, 2621, 2636, 2641,
2647, 2653, 2658, 2660, 2663, 2669, 2672, 2674–9, 2683, 2686,
2696, 2701, 2703, 2707, 2717, 2719, 2723, 2726, 2733–4, 2738,
2745, 2750, 2756, 2759, 2763, 2767, 2772, 2776, 2778, 2787,
2789, 2797, 2802, 2815, 2819, 2838, 2843, 2846, 2853, 2867, 2869,
2877–8, 2886, 2891, 2904, 2912, 2916, 2924–5, 2931–2, 2939,
2943–4, 2947, 2950, 2953, 2956, 2965, 2972, 2977, 2979, 2982,
2987, 2990, 2992, 3006, 3010, 3013, 3015, 3017, 3020, 3024–6,
3028, 3030, 3033, 3036, 3039, 3044, 3046, 3052, 3056, 3058,
3069, 3072, 3074, 3082, 3092, 3094, 3103, 3106, 3112, 3115, 3119,
3120, 3122, 3124, 3126, 3131, 3136, 3141–2, 3144, 3146, 3151,
3153, 3156, 3165, 3168, 3170, 3172, 3174, 3176, 3183, 3187, 3195,
3197, 3201, 3208, 3211–12, 3215, 3218, 3221, 3223, 3225, 3228,
3231, 3234, 3236, 3240, 3247, 3250, 3257, 3263, 3265, 3274,
3276–7, 3281–2, 3286, 3289, 3292, 3295, 3297–8, 3300–1, 3311,
3314, 3317, 3320, 3326–7, 3331, 3334–5, 3339–40, 3342, 3346, 3349,
3354–5, 3360, 3363, 3368, 3370, 3373, 3378–9, 3382, 3386–7, 3393,
3396, 3401, 3405, 3407, 3410, 3417, 3419, 3422, 3425, 3428, 3434,
3438, 3442, 3444, 3448, 3450, 3452, 3456, 3458, 3460, 3462, 3465,
3470–1, 3474, 3484, 3488, 3490, 3495, 3498, 3500, 3503, 3506,
3511, 3516, 3518, 3521, 3527, 3535, 3537–8, 3541, 3543, 3555,
3560, 3562, 3566, 3568, 3575, 3581, 3583–5, 3590, 3594, 3596,
3600, 3606–7, 3615, 3623, 3625, 3628, 3631, 3633, 3637, 3641,
3645, 3647, 3649, 3651, 3654, 3656, 3663, 3672, 3676, 3679, 3684–6,
3691, 3694, 3696, 3700, 3705, 3709–10, 3720, 3725, 3798, 3730–1,
3733, 3736, 3738–9, 3741, 3744, 3748–9, 3751–2, 3757, 3760–1,
3766, 3769, 3773–4, 3778, 3779, 3782, 3784, 3786, 3789, 3792,
3795, 3798, 3803, 3807, 3811, 3815, 3821, 3827, 3834, 3839, 3841,
3845–6, 3849, 3854, 3856–7, 3861, 3863, 3868, 3872, 3874, 3878,
3887–8, 3899, 3904–5, 3908, 3912, 3918–19, 3924–5, 3929, 3931,
3933, 3940, 3947–9, 3952, 3956, 3958, 3962, 3964, 3967, 3970,
3972, 3974, 3977, 3979, 3982, 3985, 3987–8, 3990, 4000–1, 4012,
4017–18, 4020–1, 4023, 4028, 4033, 4035, 4037, 4040, 4047, 4051,
4053–4, 4061, 4066, 4068, 4071, 4076, 4083, 4087, 4092, 4094,
4096, 4098, 4103–4, 4112, 4116, 4119, 4121, 4125, 4132, 4134,
4136, 4144–5, 4150–1, 4159, 4163–4, 4168, 4171, 4178, 4183, 4187,
4193, 4201, 4206–7, 4213, 4217, 4220, 4222, 4224–6, 4233, 4250,
4284, 4286–8, 4338–48, 4353–5, 4386–8, 4414.

Bülow   1827. DbL iv, 1934, pp. 407–11. See Part I, pp. 10 f.: 248, 256,
                      1068, 1251, 1817, 2170, 3394, 3729, 4199.
Carlyon-Britton   1913. See Part I, p. 44: 3119.
Christian VIII   King of Denmark (1839–48). Donation: 2411, 2758.
Clausen   1917. Axel Clausen, coin-dealer, Copenhagen. (K.P. 1361): 3076.

Curt

1858. Joseph Curt, coin-dealer, London (since 1838). See Part I, p. 44. (K.P. 294): 1003, 1013, 1390, 1405, 1446, 1560, 4009.

Devegge

See Part I, pp. 11 and 44, and Part II, p. ix *NNÅ* 1939, p. 86–101. *DbL* VI (1935), pp. 1 f. O. Devegge's *Mønt-og Medaille Samling*, ii (Copenhagen 1867): 316, 1082, 1196, 1699, 2200, 2302, 2740, 3054, 3343, 3776, 3883, 3996, 4317, 4360, 4413.

Egernsund find

1836. C. A. Holmboe: Mynter fra Middelalderen, fundne ved Egernsund (Coins from the Middle Ages, found at Egernsund). *Urd*, a Norwegian antiquarian-historical periodical I, 4 (Bergen 1837), no. 391 (B.P. 22): 3138.

Enegaard find

1862. See Part I, find no. 72 and Part II, p. x: 2–3, 340, 664, 773, 1097, 1256, 1605, 1653, 1904, 2008, 2301, 2311, 2333, 2615, 3530, 3551, 3608, 3716, 4120, 4123, 4266, 4271, 4290–1, 4298, 4300, 4304, 4401.

Enner find

1849. See Part I, find no. 65 and Part II, p. x: 6, 19, 33, 36, 49, 55–6, 66, 74, 92, 101, 105, 113, 116, 123, 140, 157, 175, 184, 188, 225, 260, 267, 294, 330, 345, 362, 391, 430, 436, 449, 451–2, 459, 468, 487, 513, 516, 522, 527, 531, 552, 555, 568, 575, 621, 623, 627, 651, 667, 669, 686, 707, 712–13, 716, 727, 774, 805, 816, 818–19, 824, 837, 860, 873–4, 884, 892–3, 919, 928–9, 947, 955–6, 962–3, 979, 984, 990, 994, 1000, 1023, 1031, 1039, 1048, 1079, 1087, 1109, 1142, 1175, 1181, 1206, 1226, 1235, 1248, 1266, 1271, 1288, 1309, 1318, 1321, 1328, 1334–5, 1340, 1344, 1349, 1363, 1375, 1377, 1413–14, 1440, 1452, 1467, 1476, 1509, 1516, 1543, 1559, 1575, 1577, 1586, 1633, 1637, 1646, 1648, 1655–6, 1670, 1675, 1678, 1682, 1690, 1693–4, 1718, 1760, 1763, 1768, 1773, 1778, 1780, 1784, 1814, 1821, 1824, 1833, 1896, 1899, 1901, 1910, 1920, 1923, 1928–9, 1935, 1954, 1968–9, 1971, 1975, 1979–80, 1984, 1987, 2009, 2020, 2026, 2028, 2032, 2035–6, 2052, 2056, 2066, 2073, 2104, 2121, 2132–3, 2180–1, 2185, 2189, 2204, 2207, 2238, 2241, 2246, 2274, 2276–7, 2285, 2294, 2296, 2353, 2355, 2363, 2384, 2397, 2420, 2426, 2438, 2461, 2464, 2473, 2477, 2490, 2493, 2517, 2519, 2533, 2540, 2578, 2580–1, 2590, 2605, 2607, 2609, 2611, 2630, 2638, 2642, 2650, 2655–6, 2657, 2680, 2699, 2732, 2735, 2741, 2746–7, 2749, 2769, 2781, 2785, 2791, 2796, 2798, 2809, 2831–2, 2839–40, 2845, 2855, 2857, 2859, 2864, 2876, 2880, 2882, 2946, 2948, 2951–2, 2955, 2961, 2976, 2978, 2984, 2988, 2991, 3000, 3032, 3034–5, 3038, 3043, 3051, 3067, 3075, 3077, 3085, 3091, 3105, 3111, 3114, 3118, 3123, 3133, 3152, 3154–5, 3163–4, 3166, 3178, 3182, 3185, 3191, 3196, 3213, 3217, 3222, 3235, 3246, 3270–1, 3273, 3285, 3290, 3303, 3309, 3315, 3318, 3362, 3376, 3384, 3391, 3412, 3416, 3440, 3445, 3453, 3461, 3475, 3479, 3487, 3494, 3519, 3536, 3540, 3552, 3612, 3614, 3627, 3652, 3703–4, 3711, 3718, 3732, 3737, 3747, 3753–4, 3763, 3810, 3819–20, 3824–5, 3831, 3833, 3840, 3875, 3892, 3895–6, 3898, 3910–11, 3923, 3932, 3934–5, 3950–1, 3966, 3980, 3989, 4013, 4019, 4034, 4045–6, 4064, 4067, 4101, 4110, 4113, 4130–1, 4133, 4139, 4142, 4154, 4165, 4175, 4177, 4181, 4185, 4188, 4197–8, 4229, 4231, 4238, 4242, 4245, 4301, 4316, 4323, 4369.

Ernst   1964. Barrister Axel Ernst, Odense (1891–1964). See *NNUM* 1951,
               pp. 37–40, 1961, pp. 57 f., 1964, pp. 109–13 (G.P. 2890): 138,
               353, 442, 511, 537, 588, 598, 710, 726, 757, 764, 887, 1131, 1257,
               1275, 1314, 1457, 1522, 1767, 1796, 1812, 1823, 1830, 1927, 1937,
               2075, 2109, 2169, 2171, 2224, 2227, 2229, 2258, 2315, 2372, 2463,
               2588, 2742, 2782, 2800, 2920, 2968, 2995, 3003, 3167, 3251, 3662,
               3768, 3850, 3865, 3893, 4014, 4118, 4179, 4243, 4283, 4333, 4415.

Fabricius   1935. Knud Fabricius (1875–1967). See Part I, p. 44 and II, p. x.
               (B.P. 1705): 1488.

Flensborg   1857. *Den slesvigske Oldsagssamling, Flensborg* (The Collection of
               Antiquities of Slesvig in Flensborg), ex collaborator Brasch.
               (B.P. 425): 3130.

Frost   Auction 1827. Hans Henrik Frost (1766–1825), principal of the
               Vaisenhus (orphanage). Auction I, 5 March 1827, auction II, 21
               January 1828: 50, 126, 191, 215, 292, 432, 907, 1203, 1292, 1429,
               1503, 1684, 1711, 1804, 1960, 1990, 2034, 2072, 2371, 2512, 2697,
               2797, 2983, 3027, 3443, 3873, 4024–5, 4274.

Fraenkel   1906. L.A. Fraenkel, Plock, Poland. (K.P. 1104): 2547.

Gartz   Auction 1901. See Part I, p. 44, Part II, p. x. (K.P. 980): 245, 310,
               517, 551, 565, 578, 639, 647, 744, 785, 1091, 1208, 1232, 1238,
               1332, 1346, 1372, 1458, 1492, 1580, 1631, 1807, 1944, 1976, 2061,
               2074, 2079, 2269, 2441, 2455, 2557, 2572, 2643, 2670, 2870,
               2980, 3065–6, 3129, 3358, 3528, 3785, 3828, 4135, 4157, 4212.

Glückstadt   1907. Isak Moses Hartvig Glückstadt (1839–1910), geheimeetatsraad
               (Privy Councillor), Bank manager. *DbL* viii, 1936, pp. 179 ff.
               (B.P. 1564): 2348.

Glückstadt   1924. Emil Raffael Glückstadt (1875–1923), Etatsraad (Councillor
               of State), Bank Manager. Auction 15 September and 17 November
               1924. *DbL* viii, 1936, pp. 174 ff. (K.P. 1590): 588, 598, 710, 1245,
               1767, 1796, 1812, 1823, 1830, 2372, 4243.

Haagerup find 1943. See Part I, find no. 91 and Part II, p. x: 305, 365–6, 374, 447,
               453, 472, 486, 498, 502, 504, 519, 609, 690, 695, 748, 779, 781–2,
               795, 797, 799, 827, 841, 889–90, 927, 932, 958, 1012, 1033, 1042,
               1081, 1119, 1177, 1209, 1227, 1247, 1280, 1311, 1316, 1337, 1361,
               1456, 1493, 1512, 1609–10, 1612, 1728, 1762, 1769, 1801, 1855,
               1859, 1906–7, 1943, 1945, 1951, 2053, 2108, 3087, 2165, 2220,
               2228, 2244, 2257, 2267, 2279, 2282, 2284, 2379, 2428, 2434, 2469,
               2502, 2513, 2524, 2527, 2568, 2600, 2659, 2751, 2764–5, 2773,
               2803, 2816, 2875, 2897, 3012, 3062, 3071, 3095–7, 3101, 3181,
               3306, 3319, 3338, 3398, 3400, 3469, 3483, 3492, 3525, 3534, 3544,
               3563, 3579, 3582, 3605, 3639–40, 3655, 3678, 3683, 3812, 3816,
               3867, 3889, 3999, 4050, 4107, 4214–16, 4235, 4258, 4374, 4384,
               4391, 4407, 4411.

Hartvig   Auction 1857. Mann Hartvig, genannt von Essen (1771–1838),
               merchant in Copenhagen and Hamburg. See Part I, p. 11, note 2,
               and *NNUM* 1947, pp. 138 f. Auction in Hamburg, 4 November
               1857. (K.P. 273): 777, 2539, 2748.

Hauberg   Auction 1929. Part I, pp. 19 f., 44. Part II, p. x. (K.P. 1715): 99,
               317, 442, 511, 537, 546, 558, 584, 681, 703, 746, 764, 855, 864,

1038, 1131, 1257, 1351, 1457, 1535, 1539, 1596, 1661, 1673, 1688, 1739, 1746, 1930, 1961, 2044, 2193, 2211, 2236, 2330, 2350, 2356, 2382, 2414, 2427, 2450, 2584, 2619, 2775, 2790, 2804, 2830, 2835, 2849, 2860, 2940, 2998, 3008, 3031, 3055, 3205, 3688, 3699, 4029–30, 4260–1, 4319, 4333, 4408–9.

Hede   1946. Holger Hede (1895–), barrister, Copenhagen. (G.P.2231): 348.

Heiberg   1863. Johan Ludvig Heiberg (1854–1928), schoolboy, later professor of the university, *DbL* ix, 1936, pp. 560–7, (B.P. 577): 3395.

Herbst   1854. Christian Frederik Herbst (1818–1911), keeper of Coins and Medals, Royal Collection. See Part I, p. 45, Part II, p. xi, *NFM* iii, no. 7, June 1919, pp. 87 f. (B.P. 305): 13, 3230.

Hess   Auction 1891, Adolph Hess, coin dealer, Frankfurt a. M. See Part I, p. 45, Part II, p. xi. (K.P. 785–6): 240, 484, 891, 987, 1098, 1240, 1529, 1545, 1642, 2149, 2240, 2871, 2888, 2900, 2957, 2985, 3158, 3259, 3727, 3734, 3762, 3800, 3818, 3842, 3899, 3973, 4006, 4039, 4041,

Himmelev find   1891. See Part I, find no. 49: 218.

Hoffmann   1864. Joan Henri Hoffmann (1823–97), coin dealer, Paris. (K.P. 434): 4268.

Holm   1955. Johan Chr. Holm (1914–), coin dealer, Copenhagen. (B.P. 1811): 4313.

Kelstrup find   1859. See Part I, find no. 57, and Part II, p. xii: 7, 40, 42, 57, 112, 118, 120, 144, 174, 197, 213, 228, 242, 249, 251, 254, 257, 287, 300, 375, 405–6, 410, 414, 428–9, 431, 470, 491, 564, 567, 570, 610, 629, 724, 760, 769, 791, 806, 811, 814, 843, 854, 858, 876, 904, 906, 924, 935, 937–8, 944, 972, 976, 989, 993, 999, 1009, 1014, 1016, 1041, 1043, 1045, 1059, 1064, 1067, 1070, 1072, 1074, 1094, 1096, 1107–8, 1110, 1115–17, 1123, 1143, 1153, 1172, 1180, 1183, 1188, 1204, 1236, 1242, 1272–3, 1278–9, 1293–4, 1325, 1336, 1348, 1357–9, 1365–6, 1381, 1406–7, 1418, 1420, 1462, 1466, 1472–3, 1481, 1506, 1513, 1540, 1544, 1550–1, 1583, 1605, 1667, 1696, 1740, 1752, 1757–8, 1764, 1770, 1776, 1783, 1805, 1811, 1832, 1842, 1851, 1880, 1884, 1914, 1957, 1982, 1993, 1998, 2005, 2029, 2043, 2047, 2049, 2051, 2058, 2076, 2098, 2099, 2102, 2118, 2135, 2139, 2150–2, 2153, 2184, 2206, 2213, 2249, 2270, 2303, 2319, 2335, 2339–40, 2342, 2351, 2357, 2366, 2388–9, 2391, 2393, 2395, 2398, 2401–2, 2443, 2449, 2491, 2495, 2503, 2508, 2518, 2521, 2541, 2548, 2551–2, 2556, 2558, 2577, 2612, 2616, 2627, 2727, 2736, 2768, 2805, 2841, 2872, 2881, 2885, 2892, 2894–5, 2898, 2907–8, 2938, 2949, 2975, 2986, 2993, 2996, 2999, 3004–5, 3048, 3070, 3088, 3090, 3102, 3108, 3110, 3113, 3121, 3127, 3148–50, 3161–2, 3171, 3177, 3184, 3192–3, 3245, 3255, 3261, 3308, 3330, 3351, 3369, 3381, 3392, 3403–4, 3441, 3451, 3505, 3508, 3514–15, 3517, 3520, 3554, 3556, 3602, 3714, 3717, 3721, 3726, 3735, 3790, 3801, 3805, 3809, 3823, 3838, 3843, 3847–8, 3855, 3862, 3866, 3877, 3884, 3894, 3907, 3913, 3915–16, 3937, 3946, 3969, 3991, 4022, 4043, 4055, 4074, 4077, 4100, 4129, 4141, 4143, 4156, 4223, 4227–8, 4262, 4265, 4272–3, 4297, 4303, 4306, 4321–2, 4349–52.

Kirchhoff

1902. Eiler Hagbarth Kirchhoff (1855–1922), coin-dealer, Copenhagen. *NFM* vi, no. 15, November 1922, p. 211. Part II, p. xii. (B.P. 1514): 3593.

1904. (B.P. 1534): 4253.

1916. (K.P. 1326): 272, 387, 571, 1075, 1113, 1174, 1352, 1611, 1837, 1988, 2045, 2054, 2223, 2332, 2597, 2737, 2753–4, 2760, 2808, 2814, 2844, 2918–19, 2971, 3001, 3011, 3022, 3064, 3214, 3252, 3284, 3288, 3531, 3624, 3657, 4027, 4062, 4152, 4234, 4277.

1922. (K.P. 1523): 1889, 4007.

Kirke Værløse find

1929. See Part I, find no. 97 and Part II, p. xii: 53, 652, 1323, 1967, 2595.

Kongsø plantage find

1904. See Part I, find no. 74 and Part II, p. xii: 115, 141, 170, 258, 299, 341, 380, 593, 602, 719, 723, 725, 770, 783, 852, 899, 908, 914, 1011, 1090, 1120, 1289, 1415, 1557, 1621, 1625, 1719, 1724, 1744, 1843–4, 2030, 2112, 2287, 2494, 2645, 2649, 2666, 2710–11, 2729, 2799, 2848, 2964, 3060, 3573, 3677, 4084, 4205, 4209–10, 4310, 4365.

Lassen

Adam Alexander Frederik Lassen (1788–1875), the owner of Æbeltoft pharmacy 1815–30. *DbL* xiv, 1938, p. 95. (The unknown 'P. Lassen' *NNÅ* 1949 p. 15): 507, 3468.

Lindberg

1835. Jacob Christian Lindberg (1797–1857), numismatist. Rector in Tinglev, Falster, 1844–57. *DbL* xiv, 1938, pp. 366–9. (G.P. 21): 4362.

Loscombe

Auction 1855. C. W. Loscombe of Clifton. See Part I, p. 45. (K.P. 213): 68.

Louns find

1870. See Part I, find no. 71: 597, 601, 1497, 2718, 3353, 4038.

Ludwiszcze find

Auction 1934. Dr. Richard Gaettens: *Der Fund von Ludwiszcze. Halle* (Saale), 1934. Auction catalogue xxxxi. 11 December 1934. (K.P. 1828): 4285, 4396.

Lundberg

Auction 1844. Student J. M. Lundberg, auction in Lund, 24 April 1844: 3023, 3939.

Lupow find

1890. Dr. Emil Bahrfeldt, auction Frankfurt a. M. (Adolph Hess Nachfolger) 21 June, 1921, no. 687. Donation from L. Chr. Petersen, Odense 1923. (G.P. 1751): 4267, 4383, 4397, 4399.

Lübeck find

1875. See Part II, p. xii: 4, 9, 16–17, 20–1, 30, 37, 39, 41, 48, 61, 65, 67, 72–3, 88, 90, 98, 103–4, 108, 111, 119, 124–5, 132–3, 135, 137, 148, 151–3, 163–5, 172, 177–8, 180–1, 183, 186, 190, 192, 199, 203–6, 208, 211–12, 216, 219, 221, 224, 230A, 233–4, 238, 252, 264–6, 270, 273, 277, 279, 281–2, 284, 286, 288, 308, 323, 326–9, 331, 334, 336, 338, 342–3, 346–7, 349, 351–2, 357, 359, 361, 364, 367–8, 370, 372, 376, 379, 381, 384, 385, 388–90, 397–8, 400, 408, 425, 445, 457, 461–2, 466, 469, 471, 477, 479, 488–90, 492–3, 495, 499–501, 508, 515, 524, 530, 538, 550, 556, 563, 573, 577, 580, 582, 587, 590–1, 605–7, 620, 628, 630, 637, 641–2, 646, 648–9, 654–5, 657–9, 668, 674–5, 678, 684–5, 689, 693, 696, 698, 701, 704–5, 728, 740, 745, 749–50, 758–9, 763, 775, 786–7, 793, 798, 800, 808–10, 820, 832, 835, 839, 842, 847, 859, 861, 868, 872, 878, 880, 896–8, 902, 905, 911, 916–17, 921, 926, 940, 948–9, 953, 965, 967, 971, 973, 975, 992, 1021, 1027, 1049, 1052, 1069, 1076–7, 1092, 1099,

1100, 1102–3, 1128, 1133 4, 1136, 1140, 1144, 1148, 1151, 1154 5,
1157, 1161–3, 1166–7, 1170–1, 1187, 1189, 1195, 1200, 1207, 1210,
1212, 1214, 1216–17, 1222, 1250, 1255, 1259, 1267–9, 1283, 1287,
1298, 1300–3, 1307, 1322, 1326, 1333, 1342, 1347, 1354–6, 1369,
1371, 1378, 1384, 1387, 1392, 1403, 1411, 1423, 1432–4, 1436,
1442, 1444, 1449–50, 1470–1, 1474, 1477, 1484, 1491, 1495–6,
1499, 1501, 1521, 1526–8, 1536, 1538, 1542, 1558, 1562, 1571,
1574, 1587, 1590–1, 1594–5, 1600, 1602–3, 1606–8, 1614, 1616–18,
1623–4, 1630, 1632, 1636, 1639, 1644, 1650, 1652, 1677, 1679,
1683, 1689, 1704, 1705, 1707, 1710, 1714, 1727, 1730, 1732–4,
1737, 1750–1, 1753, 1788–90, 1797, 1799, 1802, 1808, 1810, 1816,
1827, 1835–6, 1840, 1848, 1850, 1852, 1856–8, 1860–1, 1864, 1871,
1873, 1875–6, 1881, 1886, 1892, 1902, 1909, 1918, 1931, 1933,
1936, 1946, 1948–9, 1963, 1965, 1970, 1972, 1981, 1989, 1996,
2000, 2006, 2016–17, 2022–3, 2033, 2055, 2062, 2082, 2090, 2092,
2094, 2105, 2110, 2114, 2124, 2141–4, 2146, 2157, 2162, 2173–4,
2178, 2191, 2194–5, 2208, 2210, 2212, 2217, 2219, 2225–6, 2232–3,
2253, 2262, 2273, 2283, 2286, 2288, 2298–9, 2304, 2306, 2309–10,
2320–3, 2326–7, 2331, 2336, 2360, 2362, 2369, 2374, 2378, 2399,
2400, 2404, 2419, 2421, 2429–30, 2432, 2435, 2444, 2447, 2451,
2457, 2459–60, 2475, 2479, 2481, 2484, 2485, 2487–8, 2496–7,
2501, 2534, 2536, 2538, 2545, 2553, 2564–5, 2571, 2575, 2589,
2592–4, 2598, 2623–4, 2628, 2631–2, 2635, 2637, 2639–40, 2644,
2648, 2661–2, 2664–5, 2671, 2682, 2688–90, 2692, 2694–5, 2698,
2700, 2702, 2708, 2712, 2715–16, 2721, 2724, 2730–1, 2755, 2757,
2761–2, 2783–4, 2786, 2792, 2794, 2811, 2818, 2824–9, 2837, 2842,
2851–2, 2854, 2858, 2865–6, 2868, 2873, 2879, 2887, 2899, 2901–3,
2905–6, 2910–11, 2913, 2915, 2921, 2923, 2927–8, 2930, 2933,
2945, 2954, 2959, 2966, 2969, 2981, 3002, 3007, 3014, 3021, 3029,
3041–2, 3053, 3063, 3086, 3093, 3098–3100, 3104, 3117, 3128,
3132, 3137, 3143, 3145, 3186, 3200, 3202, 3204, 3207, 3220, 3229,
3238, 3241–4, 3249, 3254, 3256, 3262, 3264, 3266, 3272, 3275,
3278, 3280, 3283, 3299, 3304–5, 3310, 3312–13, 3316, 3322–3,
3329, 3333, 3341, 3344, 3348, 3357, 3359, 3361, 3365, 3383, 3388,
3406, 3413, 3421, 3424, 3429–31, 3435, 3437, 3439, 3463, 3466,
3473, 3477, 3481, 3485–6, 3504, 3509, 3512, 3524, 3526, 3532,
3545, 3550, 3553, 3559, 3565, 3572, 3574, 3576–8, 3580, 3586–8,
3597, 3601, 3609–11, 3618–19, 3622, 3626, 3630, 3634–6, 3642,
3646, 3648, 3653, 3660, 3665–6, 3673, 3675, 3681, 3706, 3715,
3722, 3740, 3756, 3759, 3771–2, 3777, 3781, 3787, 3793, 3796–
7, 3806, 3826, 3830, 3832, 3864, 3869–70, 3882, 3902–3, 3920,
3922, 3926–7, 3938, 3942–5, 3954, 3959–60, 3963, 3965, 3981,
3983–4, 3994–5, 3998, 4002–5, 4010–11, 4026, 4036, 4048–9,
4052, 4056–8, 4060, 4063, 4069, 4080–1, 4090–1, 4093, 4099,
4108–9, 4111, 4115, 4124, 4127, 4149, 4169–70, 4173, 4191–2,
4195, 4202, 4204, 4208, 4211, 4218–19, 4230, 4237, 4244, 4247,
4254–5, 4269–70, 4281–2, 4307, 4312, 4314–15, 4375, 4398.

Lyngby find   1861. See Part I, find no. 95A and Part II, p. xii: 63, 200, 202, 303,
401, 480, 755, 767, 1218, 1338, 1447, 1464, 1568, 1697, 1985,

2087, 2160, 2728, 2821, 2834, 2989, 3079, 3325, 3364, 3459, 3513, 3546, 3548, 3860, 3890, 3928.

Magnus 1868. Per Magnus, merchant in Stockholm and Berlin (c. 1833–1873). See Part I, p. 45. (G.P. 611): 751, 1080, 1561, 1660, 4182.

Mohr Auction 1847. August Christian Mohr (1775–1845), consul, chief warcommissary, Bergen. Auction 4 October 1847, Copenhagen. (K.P. 23): 291, 378, 1046, 1165, 1199, 1285, 1455, 1803, 2158, 2230, 2245, 2281, 2456, 2505, 2673, 2838, 4416.

Munksjørup find 1829. See Part I, find no. 100 and Part II, p. xiii: 159, 313, 465, 505, 592, 794, 1229, 1286, 1831, 1890, 1956, 2111, 2242, 2292, 2668, 2780, 3180, 3188, 3775, 4367, 4410.

Moller 1925. Shipowner Andr. T. Moller, Edinburgh. (K.P. 1616): 562, 618, 2346, 2507.

Monrad Peter Johan Monrad (1758–1834) Cancelli deputeret (deputy of the chancellery): 3269.

Naumann 1846, 1847, Christian Naumann (1810–88), academy secretary 1841–52, later professor juris in Lund 1852–60. (B.P. 126, 141): 10, 3783.

Nielsen 1853. Chandler Nielsen's widow, Roskilde. She is mentioned NNÅ 1949, p. 15. (B.P. 234): 869, 1761, 2168, 3632, 3799.

No Provenance 1, 32, 69, 95–7, 106, 127, 198, 236, 247, 312, 321, 354, 356, 358, 419, 423, 544, 632–3, 644, 660–1, 672, 699, 789, 867, 895, 968, 1050, 1086, 1126, 1138, 1149, 1205, 1264, 1281, 1339, 1438, 1479, 1505, 1524, 1569, 1585, 1626, 1651, 1662, 1664, 1676, 1701, 1708, 1950, 1974, 1986, 2013, 2021, 2060, 2064, 2100, 2115, 2125, 2128, 2131, 2134, 2137–8, 2215, 2251–2, 2289, 2313, 2392, 2452, 2480, 2483, 2499, 2555, 2613, 2667, 2693, 2705, 2720, 2779, 2806, 2810, 2817, 2822, 2833, 2836, 2847, 2856, 2862, 2909, 2970, 3061, 3084, 3140, 3179, 3210, 3216, 3233, 3267, 3279, 3291, 3294, 3347, 3389, 3414–15, 3418, 3427, 3446, 3472, 3547, 3599, 3603, 3638, 3644, 3698, 3702, 3750, 3764, 3829, 3997, 4105, 4117, 4138, 4180, 4203, 4239, 4257, 4295–6, 4326–8, 4335, 4366, 4370, 4380, 4392, 4395, 4406.

Overby Lyng find 1865, See Part I, find no. 58: 1485, 2048, 2691, 3659.

Petersen Auction 1917. Lauritz Christian Petersen (1859–1927), tanner, Odense. Auction I, 21 May 1917 (II, 4 May 1914). Also see NFM x, October 1927, pp. 259–61. (K.P. 1350): 52, 322, 473, 1246, 1703, 2070, 2081, 3119, 3301, 3368, 3372, 3564, 4166, 4402.

Petersen 1923. (G.P. 1751). See Bahrfeldt and Lupow find.

Purchased 1842. (B.P. 62): 54, 434.
1854. (B.P. 305): 697, 720, 964, 1004.
1856. (B.P. 379, 393): 1508, 2202.
1858. (B.P. 449): 1400.
1879. (K.P. 624): 458, 1887.
1886. (B.P. 1142): 1228.

R & D Ramus and Devegge's unfinished work on Danish medieval numismatics, see Part I, p. 11: 5, 50, 59, 117, 126, 130, 150, 191, 207, 215, 223, 248, 256, 260, 290, 292–3, 386, 395, 432, 440, 446, 464, 540, 548, 579, 595, 614, 619, 635, 650, 665, 714, 743, 756, 803, 826, 833, 881, 883, 885, 907, 1029, 1036, 1063, 1068, 1139, 1141, 1198,

1203, 1224, 1234, 1244, 1251, 1262, 1284, 1292, 1306, 1330, 1360,
1385, 1388, 1394, 1398, 1401, 1422, 1427, 1429, 1445, 1448, 1461,
1465, 1531, 1549, 1711, 1723, 1747, 1793, 1804, 1817, 1828, 1831,
1834, 1867–8, 1916, 1938, 1952, 1960, 1990, 2034, 2083, 2093,
2097, 2103, 2116, 2120, 2156, 2170, 2199, 2254, 2261, 2292, 2347,
2358, 2371, 2377, 2387, 2390, 2408, 2413, 2512, 2550, 2610, 2629,
2646, 2654, 2685, 2687, 2697, 2748, 2766, 2793, 2797, 2813, 2936,
2941, 2967, 2972, 2983, 2994, 3027, 3073, 3078, 3109, 3116, 3134,
3173, 3224, 3227, 3239, 3248, 3258, 3269, 3321, 3337, 3345, 3390,
3394, 3443, 3455, 3467, 3501, 3510, 3529, 3533, 3542, 3571, 3591,
3682, 3729, 3743, 3835–6, 3873, 3891, 3917, 3921, 3971, 4024–5,
4095, 4097, 4106, 4122, 4126, 4137, 4148, 4158, 4199, 4232, 4241,
4248–9, 4259, 4264, 4274, 4278–80, 4292–4, 4309, 4311, 4325,
4367, 4372–3, 4379, 4381–2, 4389–90, 4403, (4406).

Ready	Auction 1920. See Part I, p. 46: 51, 670.
Rollin	1856. See Part I, p. 46, Part II, p. xiii. (K.P. 229): 1192, 3377, 3380, 3670, 3680.
	1862. (K.P. 400): 3955.
Rosendalegaard find	1846. See Part I, find no. 64: 2214.
Roskilde find	1838. See Part I, find no. 80: 2316, 3402.
	1959. See Part I, find no. 54: 3755.
Sanct Jørgensbjerg find	1954. See Part I, find no. 67: 528, 1393, 1409, 1978, 2354, 2743, 3198, 3598, 3804, 4305, 4324, 4334, 4357–8, 4378, 4385.
Sandø find	1863. C. F. Herbst: *Sandö Fundet.* Ann. f.n. O. 1863, pp. 376–93 (F.P. 246): 2119, 2325, 3617, 3852.
Scharp	Auction 1853. Johan Scharp (1785–1850), merchant. Auction II, Stockholm, 9 April 1853: 2478, 2576, 2924, 3918.
Schou	Auction 1926, 7 April. Hans Henrik Schou (1858–1932), manager (A/S Atlas 1899–1920). *NFM* x, pp. 42 ff., xiii, 7 September 1932, pp. 89–91 (obituary). (K.P. 1631): 315, 512, 866, 1588, 1720, 2012, 2071, 2084, 2752, 2823.
Schubart	Auction 1831, 3 October. Carl Friderik Schubart (1797–1830), printer at the Royal Orphanage. 595, 1224, 1429, 1711, 2034, 2371, 3027, 3078, 3529, 3743, 3836.
Silkeborg Museum	1961. (B.P. 1562): 1111.
Siökrona	1883. Part I, p. 46, Part II, p. xiii. (G.P. 888): 46, 76, 139, 232, 246, 269, 411, 422, 455, 478, 586, 679, 812, 931, 942, 954, 980, 1026, 1044, 1241, 1478, 1533, 1555–6, 1579, 1615, 1634, 1713, 1826, 1908, 1919, 1966, 2205, 2235, 2442, 2462, 2466, 2528, 2543, 2770, 2774, 3006–7, 3135, 3386, 3423, 3480, 3522, 3621, 3690, 3813, 3881, 3901, 3975, 4044, 4140, 4299, 4356.
Skellegaard find	1871. See Part I, find no. 59: 3589.
Sorterup	Auction 1856. See Part II, p. xiii. (K.P. 230): 187, 1093, 1370, 1376, 1535, 3620.
Stenløse church find	Before 1922. See Part I, find no. 52: 2498.
Stockholm	1846. Kgl. Myntkabinettet, Stockholm. (B.P. 118): 81, 857, 1459, 2523, 2788, 3157, 3169, 3203, 3569, 3658, 3953.
	1854. See Part II, p. xiii. (B.P. 281): 83, 128, 158, 306, 356, 612, 687, 801, 813, 886, 903, 1373, 1389, 1402, 1408, 1628, 1635, 1685,

1853, 2002, 2259, 2352, 2367, 2375, 2381, 2424, 2500, 2510, 2525, 2554, 2569, 2734, 3016, 3052, 3069, 3567, 3697, 3851, 3885.

1856. See Part II, p. xiv. (B.P. 370): 534, 671, 1564, 1781, 1995, 2007, 2278, 2368, 2542, 2567, 2626, 3068.

1861. (B.P. 538): 201, 634, 737, 765, 1396, 1482, 1888, 1897, 3089, 2445, 2546, 3296, 3758, 3791, 4016, 4146, 4221, 4276.

1885. (B.P. 1124): 155, 176, 210, 460, 831, 939, 961, 970, 985, 1051, 1055, 1062, 1084, 1258, 1260, 1299, 1320, 1386, 1397, 1416, 2018, 2127, 2271, 2337, 2376, 2383, 2431, 2514, 2583, 2599, 2603, 2801, 2890, 2896, 2917, 2926, 2934, 2958, 3083, 3287, 3366, 3497, 3499, 3557, 3724, 3788, 3822, 3906, 4042, 4073.

1887. (B.P. 1186): 26, 2077, 2962, 4148.

Stolpehuse find 1837. See Part I, find no. 95 and Part II, p. xiv: 71, 75, 113, 147, 253, 275, 295, 302, 371, 510, 566, 691, 694, 732, 877, 1106, 1202, 1220, 1237, 1295, 1305, 1523, 1578, 1686, 1845, 1903, 1913, 2096, 2183, 2344, 2418, 2437, 2511, 2560, 2573, 2579, 2586, 2633, 2709, 2714, 2795, 3045, 3669, 3745, 4072, 4102, 4167, 4236, 4251, 4361.

Store Frigaard find 1928. See Part I, find no. 106 and Part II, p. xiv: 89, 589, 653, 918, 941, 1006, 1191, 1297, 1915, 1955, 2011, 2386, 3408, 3671, 3713, 4161, 4263, 4275, 4331–2.

Store Valby find 1839. See Part I, find no. 82 and Part II, p. xiv: 15, 25, 34, 44, 143, 161, 168, 185, 195, 230–1, 243, 262, 362, 404, 416, 438, 443, 467, 474, 476, 532, 560, 572, 583, 585, 603, 622, 626, 640, 677, 700, 711, 717, 730, 735, 752, 762, 772, 822, 848, 850, 888, 913, 922, 934, 946, 978, 988, 1007, 1010, 1018–19, 1057, 1112, 1124, 1129, 1147, 1184, 1186, 1194, 1231, 1276, 1327, 1368, 1379, 1382, 1404, 1413, 1440, 1453, 1480, 1511, 1517, 1519, 1546, 1548, 1566, 1581, 1598, 1643, 1645, 1668, 1681, 1691, 1706, 1729, 1735, 1741, 1755, 1771, 1775, 1779, 1795, 1798, 1815, 1819, 1847, 1862, 1866, 1872, 1877, 1882, 1911, 1941, 1992, 2039, 2059, 2068–9, 2080, 2129, 2166, 2176, 2188, 2222, 2256, 2266, 2295, 2297, 2317, 2365, 2370, 2407, 2422, 2425, 2446, 2448, 2465, 2467, 2471–2, 2489, 2506, 2509, 2516, 2529–30, 2561, 2566, 2596, 2602, 2620, 2622, 2625, 2651, 2684, 2704, 2739, 2744, 2807, 2812, 2874, 2883, 2893, 2914, 2922, 2935, 2937, 2942, 3009, 3040, 3047, 3049–50, 3125, 3147, 3159–60, 3175, 3199, 3302, 3307, 3332, 3336, 3356, 3367, 3409, 3489, 3491, 3493, 3496, 3507, 3558, 3595, 3616, 3629, 3650, 3667, 3674, 3687, 3689, 3692, 3701, 3712, 3742, 3765, 3802, 3909, 3957, 3961, 3976, 3986, 4015, 4032, 4059, 4065, 4078–9, 4088, 4114, 4128, 4155, 4190, 4194, 4200, 4289, 4302, 4308, 4320, 4336–7, 4368, 4376–7, 4405.

Strøby find 1868. See Part I, find no. 85 and Part II, p. xiv: 94, 1158, 2453, 3219, 4085, 4364.

Strøyberg 1839. See Part II, p. xiv. (G.P. 68): 297, 2416, 2706, 3613, 3879.

Suhm Auction 1802: Numophylacium Suhmianum II, Auction 1 June 1802. See Part I, pp. 8–9. *DbL* xxiii, 1942, pp. 114–24: 559, 595, 743, 803, 826, 2103, 3501, 3743.

Thomsen See Part I, pp. 11–17, 46 and Part II, p. xiv. *DbL* xxiii, 1942, pp. 550–6. *Catalogue . . .*, II partie, tome iii, Copenhagen, 1876: 5, 23, 28, 80, 122, 129–30, 207, 239, 274, 280, 324, 402, 464, 483,

496, 521, 533, 581, 597, 604, 613–4, 683, 721, 739, 754, 778, 802,
815, 823, 844, 901, 951, 960, 983, 1017, 1025, 1047, 1054, 1065,
1078, 1088, 1105, 1118, 1178, 1193, 1507, 1252, 1262, 1282, 1312,
1329, 1345, 1362, 1374, 1391, 1399, 1410, 1417, 1454, 1487, 1504,
1515, 1532, 1554, 1565, 1593, 1649, 1658–9, 1687, 1692, 1731,
1736, 1745, 1766, 1883, 1894, 1925, 1940, 1962, 2004, 2040, 2042,
2046, 2101, 2145, 2154–5, 2159, 2177, 2186, 2197, 2250, 2255,
2261, 2275, 2308, 2349, 2387, 2403, 2409, 2413, 2423, 2468, 2492,
2526, 2532, 2537, 2544, 2562–3, 2582, 2591, 2634, 2647, 2681,
2713, 2719, 2777, 2793, 2861, 2877, 2889, 2929, 2939, 2941, 2956,
2960, 2963, 2972, 2997, 3018, 3057, 3080–1, 3100A, 3106, 3134,
3151, 3190, 3194, 3224, 3237, 3253, 3268, 3293, 3328, 3350, 3352,
3371, 3374–5, 3379, 3385, 3397, 3410–11, 3426, 3432, 3454, 3457,
3464, 3533, 3570, 3643, 3664, 3695, 3719, 3770, 3814, 3817, 3853,
3871, 3897, 3930, 3936, 3992, 4070, 4075, 4160, 4186, 4189, 4196,
4240, 4246, 4252, 4278–80, 4292–4, 4329–30, 4371, 4404, 4412.

O. Thomsen	Auction 1880. 1 October. Ove Theodor Thomsen, retired accountant in the National Bank, Copenhagen. (K.P. 635): 220, 776, 3399.
Thorlacius	Auction 1830. Børge Thorlacius (1775–1829), philologist: 2103.
Timm	Auction 1831. Court-locksmith Georg Friderich Timm. (1746–1829). Auction I, 18 July 1831: 395, 440, 540, 743, 777, 1141, 1916, 3239, 3891, 4311.
Tornegaard find	1846. See Part I, find no. 77: 3059, 3876, 4176, 4363, 4400.
Tørring find	1830. See Part I, find no. 102 and Part II, p. xiv.: 38.
Walker	Auction 1830. Johan Daniel Walker, wholesale dealer. Auction 10 May 1830: 1867, 2646.
Wolthers	1913. (B.P. 1557): 4172.

PLATE 1

B

No.	Weight Gm.	Gr.	Die axis.	Moneyer	Hild. type	no.	
ACXEÞO (AXBRIDGE)							
1	1·10	16·9	→	ÆLFRIC	E	5	R and D Tillæg TI 12*a*.
2	0·86	13·2	↓	HVNEÞINE	E	0[1]	Enegaard find 1862.
3	1·12	17·3	↑	—	E	0[1]	Enegaard find 1862.
4	1·08	16·6	↓	LEOFÞINE	H	0[1]	Lübeck find 1.
5	1·12	17·3	↓	—	I	1	R & D CCXXIV*a* (Till T I). Thomsen 9034.
ÆGLESBYRH (AYLESBURY)							
4235	1·01	156	↑	ÆDELÞ:NE	E	0[1]	Haagerup find 333. (Plate 152.)
6	0·84	12·9	→	EADÞERD	E	0[1]	Enner find 1849.
BEARDESTAPLA (BARNSTAPLE)							
7	0·99	15·3	↑	ÆLFGAR	E	7	Kelstrup find 1859.
8	1·00	15·4	↙	—	E	7	Same dies. Bruun 1.
9	1·12	17·3	↓	—	G	8	Lübeck find 2*a*.
10	1·15	17·7	↓	—	H	9	Naumann 1846.
11	1·00	15·4	↘	—	H	9	Same dies. Bruun 3.
12	1·13	17·4	←	BYRHZIE	E	12	Bruun 2.
BAÐAN (BATH)							
13	1·14	17·6	→	ÆGELÞINE	H	17	Herbst 1854.
14	1·08	16·6	→	—	H	17	Same dies. Bruun 14.
15	1·10	16·9	↓	—	H	19	Store Valby find 1839.
16	0·95	14·6	↓	ÆLFRIC	E	0	Lübeck find 3.
17	1·08	16·6	↑	—	E	0 (cf. 20)	Lübeck find 5.
18	1·16	17·9	↗	—	E	0 (cf. 20)	Same dies. Bruun 5, ex Bille-Brahe.
19	1·48	22·8	↙	—	E	21	Enner find 1849.
20	1·16	17·9	↑	—	G	0	Lübeck find 4.
21	1·14	17·6	↑	—	G	23	Lübeck find 5*a*.
22	0·98	15·1	←	—	G	23	Same dies. Bruun 12.
23	(1·03)	(15·9)	↓	—	H	25	Thomsen 9035. Chipped.
24	1·10	16·9	↓	—	H	25	Same dies. Bruun 15.
25	1·09	16·8	←	ÆLFÞINE	G	27	Store Valby find 1839. Broken.
26	1·08	16·7	↓	ÆLÞINE	H	30	Stockholm 1887.
27	0·99	15·3	↓	ÆSTAN	G	32	Bech, auction 1906, no. 34.
28	1·15	17·7	↑	ÆÐESTAN	E	36	Same dies as 29. Thomsen 9036.

[1] Moneyer not recorded by Hildebrand for the mint in this reign.

PLATE 1

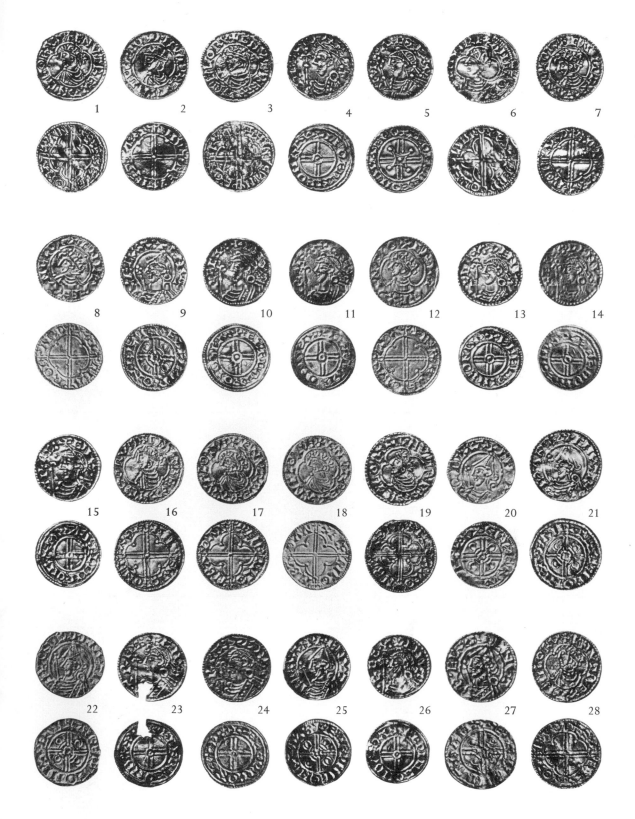

1   2   3   4   5   6   7

8   9   10   11   12   13   14

15   16   17   18   19   20   21

22   23   24   25   26   27   28

PLATE 2

No.	Weight Gm.	Gr.	Die axis	Moneyer	type	Hild no.	

BATH (*contd.*)

No.	Gm.	Gr.	axis	Moneyer	type	no.	Notes
29	1·13	17·4	↗	ÆÐESTAN	E	36	Same dies as 28. Bruun 6 ex Bille-Brahe.
30	1·15	17·7	→	—	E	cf. 36	Lübeck find 10.
31	0·94	14·5	↖	—	E	o	Bruun 7.
32	1·10	16·9	→	—	E	37	No provenance.
33	1·08	16·6	←	—	E	37	Enner find 1849.
34	1·09	16·8	←	—	G	38	Store Valby find 1839.
35	1·10	16·9	↑	—	G	38	Same dies. Bruun 13.
36	1·14	17·6	↑	—	G	cf. 39	(BAÐ) Enner find 1849.
37	0·98	15·1	↑	—	G	cf. 39	(BAÐ) (ÆÐÆSTAN) Lübeck find 6a.
38	1·12	17·3	←	—	H	o[1]	Tørring find 1830.
39	1·14	17·6	↑	—	H	o[1]	Lübeck find 8.
40	1·11	17·1	↓	ALFOLD	G	40	Kelstrup find 1859.
41	1·19	18·3	→	—	G	cf. 40	Same rev. die. Lübeck find 10a.
42	0·88	13·6	↑	ALFPALD	E	41	Kelstrup find 1859.
43	0·92	14·2	↓	—	E	41	Same dies. Bruun 10.
44	1·05	16·2	↓	—	E	42	Store Valby find 1839.
45	1·14	17·6	↓	—	E	42	Same dies. Bruun 8.
46	1·10	16·9	↘	—	E	43	Bruun 9, ex Bille-Brahe, ex Siökrona 1883. Cracked.
47	1·45	22·3	↗	ALFPOLD	E	o (cf. 45)	Bruun 11.
48	0·94	14·5	↓	—	G	46	Lübeck find 12.
49	1·15	17·7	↑	—	G	47	Enner find 1849.
50	1·10	16·9	↓	ELFRICI	B	49[3]	R & D XI. Frost, auction 1827, no. 6.
51	1·05	16·2	↗	—	B	49[3]	Same dies. Bruun 4, ex Ready, Sale, 1920, 125.
52	0·82	12·6	←	ELRIC	H	o[2]	Petersen, auction 1917, no. 66.

BEDANFORD (BEDFORD)

No.	Gm.	Gr.	axis	Moneyer	type	no.	Notes
53	1·15	17·7	↓	ÆGELMAN	H	o[1]	Kirke Værløse find 183.
54	0·99	15·3	↓	ÆGLMAN	G	o	Purchased 1842.
55	0·92	14·2	↓	ÆGLGET	E	o	Enner find 1849.
56	1·04	16·1	↑	ÆGLMAN	G	53	Enner find 1849.

[1] Moneyer not recorded by Hildebrand for the type.
[2] Moneyer not recorded by Hildebrand for the mint in this reign, unless equals Ælfric.
[3] Scandinavian?—see p. ix.

Plate 2

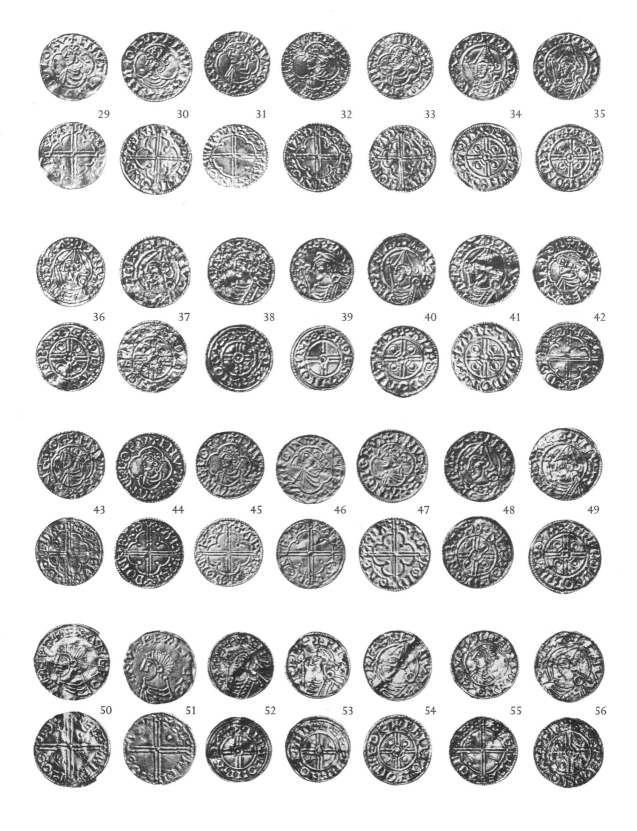

29   30   31   32   33   34   35

36   37   38   39   40   41   42

43   44   45   46   47   48   49

50   51   52   53   54   55   56

PLATE 3

No.	Weight Gm.	Gr.	Die axis	Moneyer	Hild. type	no.	
BEDFORD (contd.)							
57	1·02	15·7	↓	GODRIC	E	0 (cf. 55)	Kelstrup find 1859.
58	1·35	20·8	←	—	E	0	Bruun 16.
59	1·10	16·9	↓	GODÞINE	E	56	Same obv. die as 63–4. Beskrivelse 1791, no. 36. R & D 3.
60	1·19	18·3	↓	LEOFÞINE	E	58	Bruun 17, ex Bille-Brahe.
61	1·18	18·2	↓	—	E	cf. 58	Lübeck find (not in *Zfn*).
62	1·02	15·7	←	—	E	60	Bruun 19.
63	1·01	15·6	←	—	E	61	Same dies as 64; same obv. die as 59. Lyngby find 1861.
64	1·02	15·7	↓	—	E	0	Same dies as 63; same obv. die as 59. Bruun 18. Cracked.
65	0·95	14·6	↑	—	E	cf. 62	Lübeck find 14.
66	0·98	15·1	↖	—	E	cf. 62	Same dies. Enner find 1849.
67	1·19	18·3	→	—	G	0[1]	Lübeck find 13.
68	1·02	15·7	↓	LEOÞINE	H⎹	0[1]	Loscombe Sale 1855, 1093.
69	1·17	18·1	↓	SOTA	H	67	No provenance.
70	1·09	16·8	→	—	H	67	Same dies. Bruun 20, ex Bille-Brahe.
71	0·97	14·9	↓	SÞETE	H	0[2]	Stolpehuse find 1837.
72	1·12	17·3	↑	SÞOTA	H	0	Lübeck find 16.
BRIGGSTOW (BRISTOL)							
73	0·97	14·9	←	ÆGELÞINE	Ed	71	Same dies as 75. Lübeck find (not in *Zfn*). Broken.
74	1·10	16·9	↑	—	E	cf. 70	Same obv. die as 76. Enner find 1849.
75	0·99	15·3	→	—	Ed	cf. 71.	Same dies as 73. Stolpehuse find 1837.
76	1·00	15·4	→	—	E	cf. 70.	Same obv. die as 74. Siökrona 1883.
77	1·19	18·4	↑	—	H	73	Bonderup find 1854.
78	0·92	14·2	←	ÆGLÞINE	Ed	0 (cf. 71)	Bruun 23.
79	1·10	16·9	←	—	Ed	0 (cf. 71)	Bruun 24.
80	1·11	17·2	←	ÆLFÞINE	E	75	Same dies as 83; same obv. die as 81–2. Thomsen 9038.
81	1·15	17·8	↓	—	E	75	Same dies as 82; same obv. die as 80 and 83. No provenance.
82	1·06	16·3	↙	—	E	75	Same dies as 81; same obv. die as 80 and 83. Bruun 21.
83	1·16	17·9	↘	—	E	75	Same dies as 80; same obv. die as 81–2. Bruun 22, ex Bille-Brahe, ex Stockholm 1854.
84	0·84	12·9	→	—	Ed	79	Bruun 25.

[1] Moneyer not recorded by Hildebrand for the type.
[2] Moneyer not recorded by Hildebrand for the mint in this reign.

PLATE 3

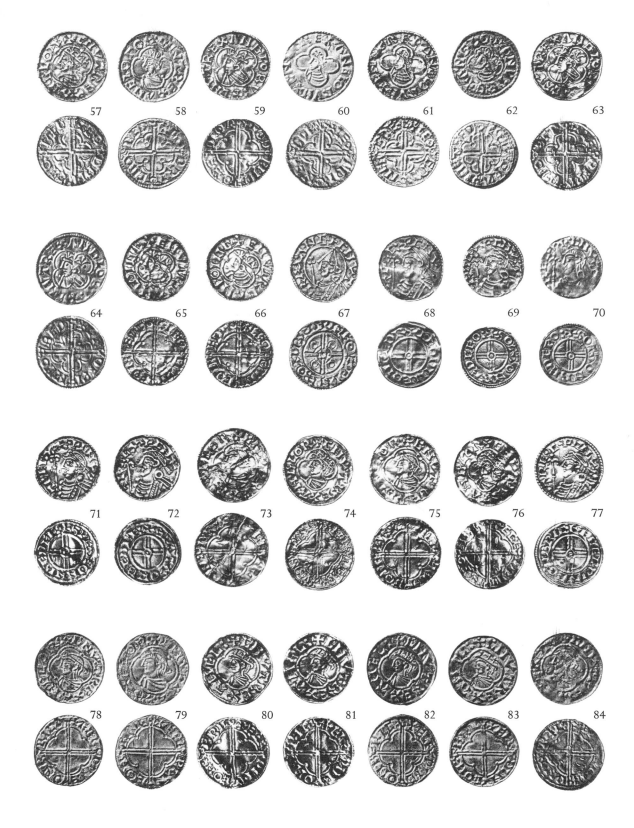

57　58　59　60　61　62　63

64　65　66　67　68　69　70

71　72　73　74　75　76　77

78　79　80　81　82　83　84

PLATE 4

No.	Weight Gm.	Gr.	Die axis	Moneyer	Hild. type	Hild. no.	
BRISTOL (*contd.*)							
85	1·04	16·1	↙	ÆLFÞINE	Ed	o	Bruun 26.
86	0·94	14·5	→	—	Ed	o	Bruun 27.
87	1·12	17·3	→	ÆÐESTAN	I	o[1]	Bruun 30.
88	0·95	14·7	←	ELFÞINE	Ed	o (cf. 75)	Lübeck find 18.
89	0·98	15·1	↑	GODAMAN	Ed	o (cf. 83)	Store Frigaard find 1928.
90	0·99	15·3	↓	LEOFÞINE	H	cf. 84	Lübeck find 19.
91	1·14	17·6	→	SÆÞINE	K	cf. 86	Bruun 32.
92	0·90	13·9	←	ÞVLFÞINE	Ed	88	Enner find 1849.
93	1·04	16·1	↓	—	I	90	Bruun 31.
94	1·07	16·5	↓	—	I	cf. 90	Same dies. Strøby find 1868.
95	1·10	16·9	→	—	I	cf. 90	No provenance.
96	1·12	17·3	←	—	I	cf. 90	No provenance.
97	0·97	14·9	←	ÞVLSTAN	H	92	No provenance.
98	0·93	14·3	↑	—	H	cf. 92	Lübeck find 24.
4415	0·52	8·1	↗	ÞYNSIGE	E	95	Ernst donation 1964. Pierced. (Plate 158.)
99	1·30	20·1	↑	—	Ed	97	Hauberg, auction 1929, 28. Cracked.
100	0·88	13·6	↗	—	Ed	97	Same dies. Bruun 28. Cracked.
101	0·86	13·3	↓	—	Ed	98	Enner find 1849.
102	0·93	14·3	↗	—	Ed	98	Bruun 29, ex Bille-Brahe.
103	0·69	10·6	→	—	Ed	98	Lübeck find 20a.
104	0·69	10·6	→	—	Ed	99	Lübeck find 20.
BRIUTUNE (BRUTON)							
105	0·99	15·3	←	ÆLFELM	G	103	Enner find 1849.
106	1·05	16·2	→	—	G	cf. 104	R & D Tillæg T I 3a.
107	0·96	14·8	↑	—	G	cf. 104	Bruun 34.
108	1·16	17·9	←	—	H	105	Lübeck find 21.
109	1·18	18·2	↙	—	H	105	Bruun 35.
110	1·03	15·9	→	—	H	105	Bruun 36.
111	0·98	15·1	↓	—	H	cf. 105	Same dies. Lübeck find 22.
112	0·79	12·2	↑	ÆLFFELM	E	cf. 106	Kelstrup find 1859.

[1] Moneyer not recorded by Hildebrand for the type nor for Cnut or Harthacnut at Bristol.

PLATE 4

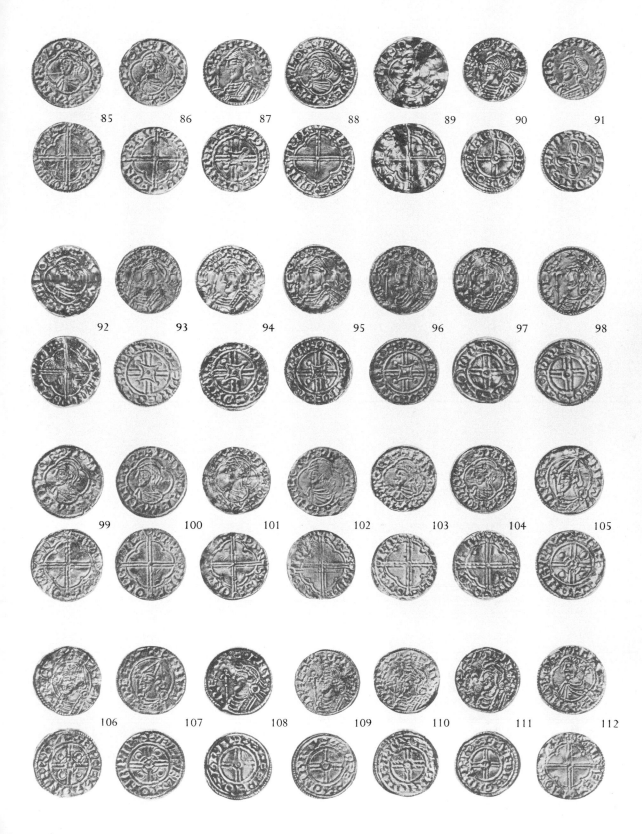

85   86   87   88   89   90   91

92   93   94   95   96   97   98

99   100   101   102   103   104   105

106   107   108   109   110   111   112

PLATE 5

No.	Weight Gm.	Gr.	Die axis	Moneyer	type	Hild. no.	
BRUTON (contd.)							
113	0·70	10·8	↑	ÆLFÞIINE	Ed	o	Same dies as 114; same obv. die as 116. Enner find 1849 or Stolpehuse find 1837.
114	0·72	11·1	→	—	Ed	o	Same dies as 113; same obv. die as 116. Bruun 33.
115	0·70	10·8	→	ÆLFÞINE	Ed	cf. 110	Kongsø plantage find 68.
116	0·65	10·1	↓	—	Ed	cf. 110	Same obv. die as 113–14. Enner find 1849.
117	1·08	16·6	→	GODRICC	I	o[1]	Beskrivelse 1791, no. 31. R & D 4.
BRYIDGE (BRIDPORT)							
118	1·04	16·1	↓	ALÞOLD	G	o[2]	Kelstrup find 1859.
119	1·11	17·1	←	—	G	o[2]	Same obv. die. Lübeck find 23.
4236	1·12	17·3	→	GODRIC	E	o[2]	Stolpehuse find 1837. (Plate 152.)
BUCCINGAHAM (BUCKINGHAM)							
120	1·25	19·3	↓	LEOFRIC	E	114	Kelstrup find 1859.
121	0·97	14·9	↖	—	E	cf. 114	Bruun 37.
122	1·16	17·9	↑	—	G	116	Thomsen 9044.
CÆNTÞARABYRH (CANTERBURY)							
123	1·03	15·9	←	ÆLFRED	G	cf. 120	Enner find 1849.
124	1·11	17·1	↑	—	H	o (cf. 121)	Lübeck find 25.
125	1·10	16·9	←	—	H	o (cf. 121)	Lübeck find 26.
126	1·07	16·5	↑	—	I	122	R & D XII. Frost, auction 1827, no. 7.
127	1.07	16·5	↓	ÆLFRIC	H	cf. 123	No provenance.
128	1·11	17·1	↓	ÆLFRYD	E	124	Stockholm 1854.
129	1.18	18·2	↙	—	E	124	Same dies. Bruun 40, ex Bille-Brahe, ex Thomsen 9046.
130	1·12	17·3	←	BRHTRED	H	129	R & D XIII. Thomsen 9047.
131	1·17	18·1	←	—	H	129	Same dies. Bruun 50.
132	1·06	16·3	↓	BRIHTRED	H	131	Lübeck find 30.
133	1·10	16·9	↓	—	H	132	Lübeck find 31.
134	1·07	16·5	↓	—	H	132	Same dies. Bruun 51.
135	1·16	17·9	↑	—	H	cf. 133	Lübeck find 33.
136	1·19	18·3	↑	—	H	cf. 133	Same dies. Bruun 52, ex Bille-Brahe.
137	0·87	13·5	←	—	H	cf. 134	Lübeck find 32.
138	1·49	23·0	→	EADÞOLD	E	135	Ernst donation 1964. Pierced.
139	1·12	17·3	→	EDÞINE	G	137	Siökrona 1883.
140	1·06	16·3	↓	—	G	cf. 137	Enner find 1849.

[1] Moneyer not recorded by Hildebrand for the type nor for Cnut or Harthacnut at Bruton.
[2] Moneyer and type not recorded by Hildebrand for the mint in this reign.

PLATE 5

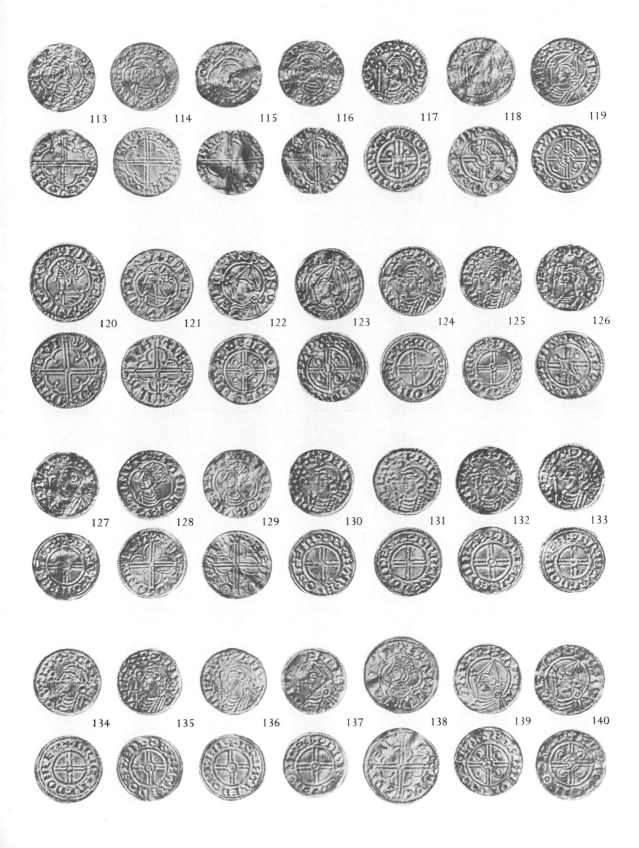

113   114   115   116   117   118   119

120   121   122   123   124   125   126

127   128   129   130   131   132   133

134   135   136   137   138   139   140

PLATE 6

No.	Weight Gm.	Gr.	Die axis	Moneyer	Hild. type	no.	

CANTERBURY (*contd.*)

No.	Gm.	Gr.	axis	Moneyer	type	no.	
1487	0·94	14·5	←	GCYLDEƿINE	I	0	Thomsen 9153. (Plate 54.)
141	1·01	15·6	↓	GODRIC	E	cf. 139	Kongsø plantage find 69.
142	1·06	16·3	↓	—	E	cf. 139.	Bech, auction 1906, no. 42.
143	1·11	17·1	↑	—	G	0[1]	Store Valby find 1839.
144	1·45	22·3	↑	LEOFNOĐ	E	0	Kelstrup find 1859.
145	1·09	16·8	→	—	E	0	Same obv. die. Benzon, donation 1885, no. 1.
146	1·04	16·1	←	—	E	0 (cf. 145)	Bruun 41.
147	1·02	15·7	↑	—	E	0 (cf. 145)	Same dies. Stolpehuse find 1837.
148	0·99	15·3	→	—	G	146	Lübeck find 36.
149	0·93	14·3	→	—	G	146	Same dies. Bruun 42.
150	1·16	17·9	↑	—	G	147	Beskrivelse, Tillæg 1794 no. 11. R & D 5.
151	1·11	17·1	↓	—	G	cf. 148	Lübeck find 37.
152	0·98	15·1	↑	—	G	149	Lübeck find (not in *ZfN*).
153	1·13	17·4	→	—	H	150	Lübeck find 34.
154	1·12	17·3	→	—	H	150	Same dies. Bruun 53, ex Bille-Brahe.
155	1·17	18·1	←	—	H	150	Stockholm 1885.
156	1·11	17·1	↑	LEOFRIC	Aa	154[3]	Bruun 39.
157	0·99	18·3	→	LEOFSTAN	E	cf. 155	Enner find 1849.
158	0·89	13·7	←	LEOFƿINE	E	0[2]	Stockholm 1854.
1298	1·06	16·4	↓	—	G	156	Same dies as Hild. 156. Lübeck find 421. (Plate 47.)
159	0·94	14·5	→	—	G	157	Same dies as 160; same obv. die as 163. Munksjørup find 1829.
160	0·96	14·8	←	—	G	157	Same dies as 159; same obv. die as 163. Bruun 43, ex Bille-Brahe.
161	0·95	14·7	↓	—	G	158	Store Valby find 1839.
162	0·93	14·3	↓	—	G	158	Bruun 44.
163	0·88	13·6	↓	—	G	(cf. 157)	Lübeck find 45.
164	0.93	14·3	→	—	G	0	Lübeck find 46.
165	0·89	13·7	↓	—	H	cf. 159	Lübeck find 41.
166	1·01	15·6	↑	—	H	159	Bruun 55.
167	1·00	15·4	→	—	H	cf. 159	Bruun 54.
168	0.88	13·6	→	—	H	161	Store Valby find 1839.

[1] Moneyer not recorded by Hildebrand for the type.
[2] Moneyer not recorded by Hildebrand for the type, unless equals Hild. 163 which is unlikely.
[3] Scandinavian?—see p. ix. (Aa = A+E).

PLATE 6

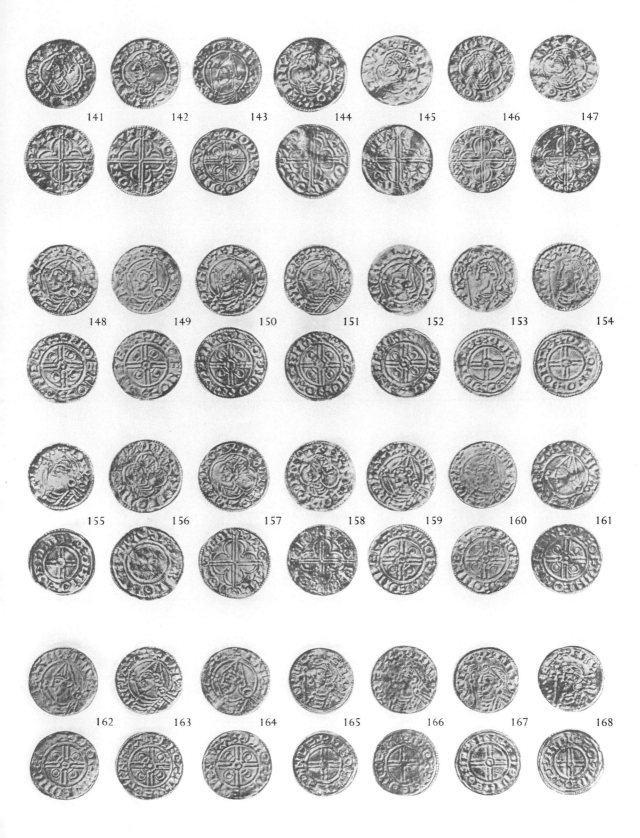

141   142   143   144   145   146   147

148   149   150   151   152   153   154

155   156   157   158   159   160   161

162   163   164   165   166   167   168

PLATE 7

No.	Weight Gm.	Gr.	Die axis	Moneyer	Hild. type	no.	
CANTERBURY (*contd.*)							
169	1·08	16·6	→	LEOFꝘINE	H	161	Bruun 56, ex Bille-Brahe.
170	1·14	17·6	←	LIOFNOÐ	E	o (cf. 165)	Kongsø plantage find 70.
171	0·86	13·2	←	—	E	o (cf. 165)	Bech, auction 1906, no. 43.
172	1·10	16·9	→	ꝘIHRED	H	168	Lübeck find 59.
173	1·10	16·9	→	—	H	168	Same dies. Bruun 58.
174	1·23	19·0	↓	ꝘIINEDÆI	E	169	Kelstrup find 1859.
175	0·86	13·2	↑	ꝘINEDÆG	G	170	Enner find 1849.
176	0·99	15·3	→	ꝘINEDÆI	G	171	Stockholm 1885.
177	1·08	16·6	→	—	G	cf. 171	Lübeck find 50.
178	0·96	14·8	→	—	G	cf. 171	Lübeck find 49.
179	1·17	18·1	→	—	G	cf. 171	Bruun 45, ex Bille-Brahe.
180	0·79	12·2	↓	—	H	172	Var. with crowned bust, cf. *NC* 1963, 93–5. Lübeck find 51.
181	1·10	16·9	→	—	H	173	Lübeck find 52.
182	1·09	16·8	→	—	H	173	Same dies. Bruun 57.
183	1·08	16·6	↓	ꝘINEDÆIG	G	174	Lübeck find 47.
184	0·99	15·3	↑	—	G	cf. 174	Enner find 1849.
185	1·08	16·6	→	—	G	cf. 174	Store Valby find 1839.
186	0·92	14·2	↑	ꝘINEDÆII	G	o	Lübeck find 53.
187	0·89	13·7	←	ꝘINEDEG	E	o	Sorterup, auction 1856, no. 459.
188	0·96	14·8	↑	ꝘINEIDÆII	G	176	Enner find 1849.
189	0·91	14·1	↓	—	G	176	Bruun 46.
190	0·99	15·3	↑	—	G	177	Lübeck find 55.
191	0·99	15·3	↓	—	G	cf. 177	Same rev. die. R & D XVII. Frost, auction 1827, no. 9.
192	1·00	15·4	←	ꝘINRÆD	G	cf. 178	Lübeck find 57.
193	0·99	15·3	→	—	G	cf. 178	Bruun 47.
194	0·92	14·2	→	ꝘINRED	G	178	Benzon, donation 1885, no. 2.
195	1·00	15·4	→	—	G	cf. 180	Store Valby find 1839.
196	0·98	15·1	→	—	G	cf. 180	Same dies. Bruun 48.

PLATE 7

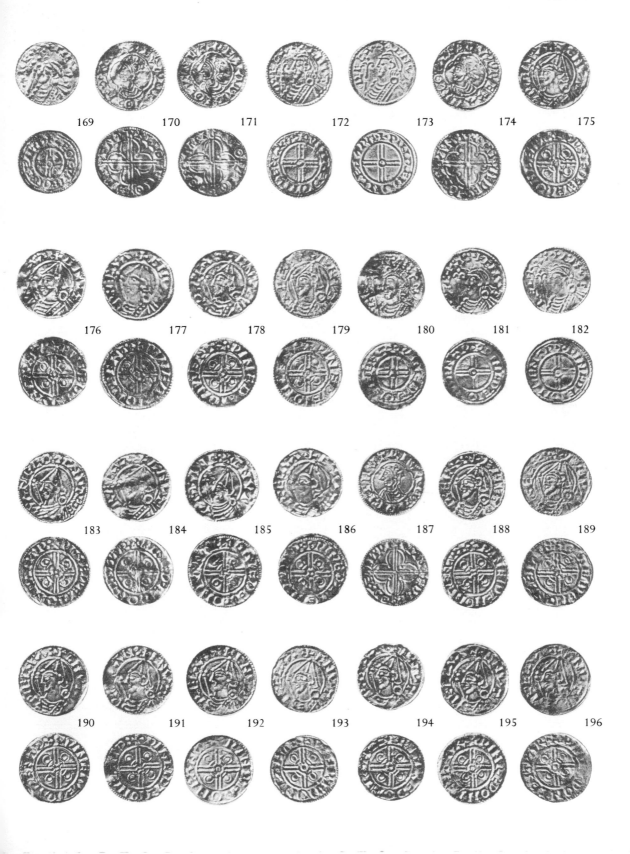

169 170 171 172 173 174 175

176 177 178 179 180 181 182

183 184 185 186 187 188 189

190 191 192 193 194 195 196

PLATE 8

No.	Weight Gm.	Weight Gr.	Die axis	Moneyer	type	Hild. no	
CANTERBURY (*contd.*)							
197	1·16	17·9	↑	ꝥINRED	G	181	Kelstrup find 1859.
198	1·14	17·6	↑	—	H	o[1]	Munksjørup find 1829. R & D Tillæg T. I no. 5c.
199	1·20	18·5	↓	—	H	o[1]	Same dies. Lübeck find 59.
200	1·16	17·9	↑	ꝥVLFSTAN	E	184	Lyngby find 1861.
201	1·13	17·4	→	—	E	184	Same dies. Stockholm 1861.
202	1·31	20·2	→	—	E	o	Lyngby find 1861.
203	0·90	13·9	→	—	G	o	Lübeck find 61.
204	1·11	17·1	↑	ꝥVLFꝥI	H	o	Lübeck find (not in *ZfN*).
205	0·90	13·9	←	ꝥVLFꝥIG	G	186	Lübeck find 62a.
206	1·50	23·1	→	—	H	cf. 187	Lübeck find 62.
207	1·15	17·7	←	ꝥVLFꝥI VBI	I	o[2]	R & D XVIII. Thomsen 9051.
208	0·99	15·3	↓	ꝥVLSTAN	G	188	Lübeck find 63.
209	1·11	17·1	→	—	G	188	Same dies. Bruun 49.
210	1·12	17·3	↓	—	G	189	Stockholm 1885.
211	1·10	16·9	↑	—	G	o	Lübeck find 65.
212	0·93	14·3	↑	—	G	o	Lübeck find 64.
213	1·05	16·2	↖	ꝥYNRED	E	191	Kelstrup find 1859.
CESꝦ . . . (CAISTOR?)							
214	1·43	22·1	↓	ÆLFSIGI	E	cf. 193	Bruun 59. Pierced.
CISECEASTER (CHICHESTER)							
215	1·12	17·3	↑	ÆGELM	G	195	R & D XIX. Frost, auction 1827, no. 10.
216	1·13	17·4	←	—	H	196	Same dies as 217 and 223. Lübeck find 66.
217	1·12	17·3	←	—	H	196	Same dies as 216 and 223. Bruun 66.
218	(0·97)	(14.9)	↑	ÆILM	G	o	Himmelev find *c.* 1891. Chipped.
219	1·12	17·3	↑	ÆLFRIC	H	cf. 198	Same obv. die as 220–1. Lübeck find 67.
220	1·00	15·4	↑	—	H	cf. 198	Same dies as 221; same obv. die as 219. Bruun 68, ex Bille-Brahe, ex O. Thomsen, auction 1880, no. 874.
221	1·12	17·3	↑	—	H	198	Same dies as 220; same obv. die as 219. Lübeck find 68.
222	1·13	17·4	↑	—	H	198	Bruun 67.
223	(0·52)	(8·1)	←	(ÆGELM)	H	196	Same dies as 216–17. R & D 7. Bonderup find 1822. Cut halfpenny.
224	1·10	16·9	↓	ÆꝦELM	E	199	Lübeck find 479 (*sic*!).

[1] Moneyer not recorded by Hildebrand for the type.
[2] This double name not recorded by Hildebrand for the type nor for Cnut or Harthacnut at Canterbury.

PLATE 8

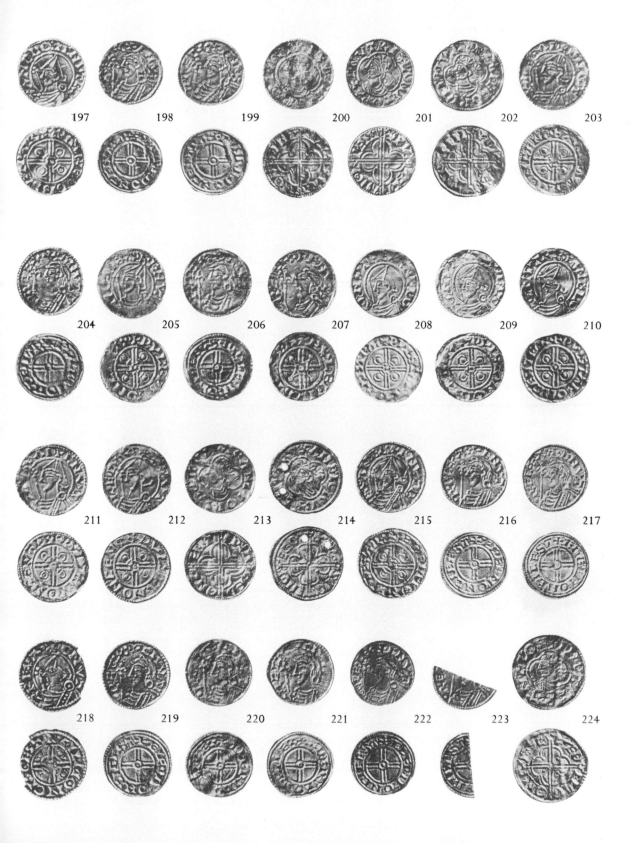

PLATE 9

D

| | Weight | | Die | | Hild. | | |
No.	Gm.	Gr.	axis	Moneyer	type	no.	

CHICHESTER (*contd.*)

No.	Gm.	Gr.	axis	Moneyer	type	no.	Provenance
225	1·12	17·3	←	ÆÐELM	E	201	Enner find 1849.
226	1·00	15·4	↙	—	E	201	Same dies. Bruun 60.
227	0·96	14·8		—	E	202	Bruun 61.
228	1·13	17·4	↓	BRIHTNOÐ	E	203	Same dies as 229–30 and 230 a. Kelstrup find 1859.
229	1·10	16·9	↗	—	E	203	Same dies as 228, 230 and 230 a. Bruun 62.
230	1·00	15·4	↑	—	E	203	Same dies as 228–9 and 230 a. Store Valby find 1839.
230a	1·18	18·2	→	—	E	203	Same dies as 228–30. Lübeck find 488. (Plate 54.)
231	1·16	17·9	←	LEOFRIC	G	206	Store Valby find 1839.
232	1·11	17·1	←	—	G	206	Bruun 64, ex Bille-Brahe, ex Siökrona 1883.
233	1·11	17·1	→	—	H	207	Lübeck find 69.
234	0·82	12·6	←	LEOFÞI	G	o[1]	Lübeck find 70.
235	0·86	13·2	↓	LEOFÞINE	E	o	Benzon, donation 1885, no. 3.
236	1·16	17·9	↑	—	G	208	No provenance.
237	1·12	17·3	↑	—	G	208	Bruun 65.
238	1·11	17·1	↑	—	G	o	Lübeck find (not in *ZfN*).
239	0·87	13·4	↓	—	H	o	Thomsen 9052.
240	1·08	16·6	←	LIOFRIC	E	209	Hess auction 1891, no. 903.
241	1·17	18·1	↘	—	E	209	Same rev. die. Bruun 63.
242	0·97	14·9	↑	ÞVLFNOÐ	E	o[2]	Kelstrup find 1859.

COLENCEASTER (COLCHESTER)

No.	Gm.	Gr.	axis	Moneyer	type	no.	Provenance
243	0·95	14·6	↙	ÆLFÞINE	E	211	Store Valby find 1839.
244	1·07	16·5	↘	—	E	211	Bruun 69.
245	1·00	15·4	↓	—	E	212	Gartz, auction 1901, no. 1158.
246	0·92	14·2	↓	—	E	212	Bruun 70, ex Bille-Brahe, ex Siökrona 1883. Broken.
247	0·88	13·6	→	—	E	213	Munksjørup find 1829. R & D Tillæg T. I no. 114 b.
248	0·79	12·2	↓	BRVNMAN	E	216	R & D XXIII. Bülow, auction 1827, no. 2.
249	0·85	13·1	→	—	E	cf. 216	Same dies. Kelstrup find 1859.
250	0·85	13·1	←	—	E	cf. 216	Same dies. Bruun 71, ex Bille-Brahe.
251	0·90	13·9	↓	—	E	217	Kelstrup find 1859.
252	1·09	16·8	↓	CODRIC	H	cf. 226	Lübeck find 74.

[1] Moneyer not recorded by Hildebrand for the mint in this reign, unless equals Leofwine.
[2] Moneyer not recorded by Hildebrand for the mint in this reign.

PLATE 9

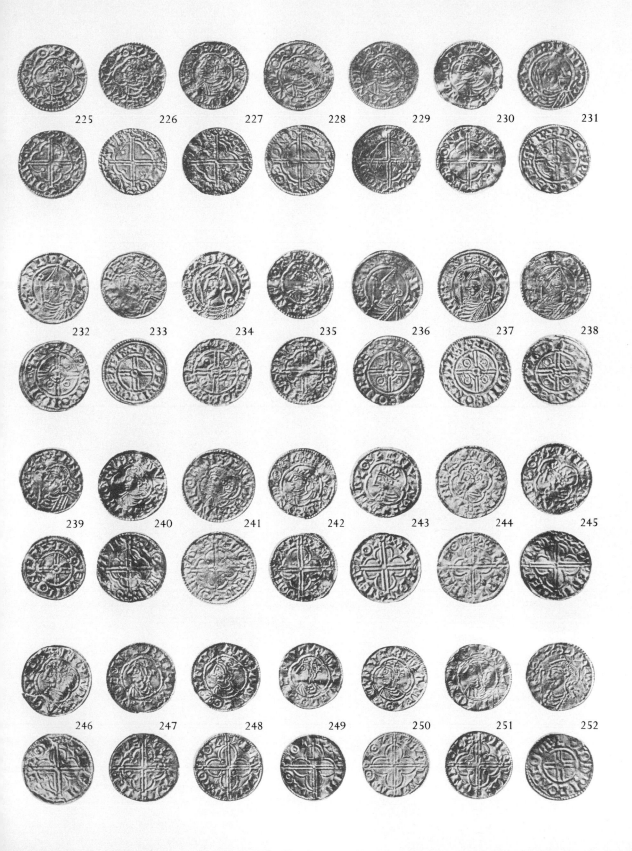

PLATE 10

No.	Weight Gm.	Gr.	Die axis	Moneyer	type	Hild. no.	

COLCHESTER (*contd.*)

No.	Gm.	Gr.	Die axis	Moneyer	type	Hild. no.	
253	0·93	14·3	↙	EDPINE	E	218	Same obv. die as 254 and 255. Stolpehuse find 1837.
254	0·92	14·2	↓	—	E	218	Same dies as 255; same obv. die as 253. Kelstrup find 1859.
255	0·95	14·6	→	—	E	218	As last. Bruun 72.
256	0·74	11·4	↓	GODRI	E	219	R & D XXIV. Bülow, auction 1827, no. 5.
257	0·98	15·1	→	GODRIC	E	221	Kelstrup find 1859.
258	0·92	14·2	←	—	E	221	Kongsø plantage find 71.
259	0·90	13·9	→	—	E	221	Bruun 73.
260	0·96	14·8	←	—	E	cf. 221	R & D 8 or Enner find 1849.
261	0·91	14·1	→	—	E	cf. 221	Bruun 74.
262	1·10	16·9	↓	—	G	223	Store Valby find 1839.
263	0·94	14·5	←	—	G	223	Same dies. Bruun 76, ex Bille-Brahe.
264	1·09	16·8	↑	—	H	0	Lübeck find 77.
265	1·12	17·3	←	—	H	227	Lübeck find 79.
266	0·78	12·1	↓	LEOFPINE	H	229	Lübeck find 81.
267	1·01	15·6	↑	PLFPINE	G	230	Enner find 1849.
268	0·97	14·9	↑	—	G	230	Same dies. Bruun 77.
269	(0·77)	(11·9)	←	PVLFPINE	E	cf. 231	Siökrona 1883. Damaged.
270	0·99	15·3	←	—	E	233	Lübeck find 83.
271	0·84	12·9	↖	—	E	233	Bruun 75, ex Bille-Brahe.
272	0·84	12·9	→	—	E	234	Kirchhoff 1916.
273	1·05	16·3	↓	—	G	236	Lübeck find 85.
274	1·11	17·1	↑	—	G	237	Thomsen 9054.
275	1·17	18·1	↑	—	H	239	Stolpehuse find 1837.
276	1·09	16·8	→	—	H	239	Same dies. Bruun 78.
277	1·19	18·3	←	—	H	cf. 240	Lübeck find 86.
278	1·17	18·1	→	—	H	cf. 240	Same dies. Bruun 79, ex Bille-Brahe.

CROCGLADE (CRICKLADE)

No.	Gm.	Gr.	Die axis	Moneyer	type	Hild. no.	
279	1·15	17·7	↑	ÆGELPINE	G	0	Lübeck find 88.
280	1·10	16·9	←	—	H	0[1]	Thomsen 9056, ex Munksjørup find 1829. R & D Tillæg T. I no. XXIV, *a*.

[1] Moneyer not recorded by Hildebrand for the type.

PLATE 10

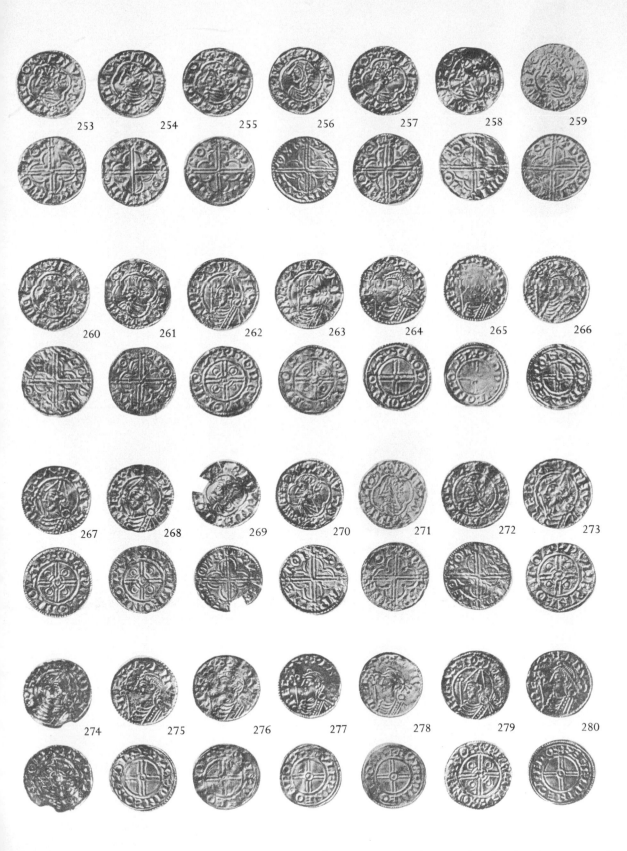

253 254 255 256 257 258 259

260 261 262 263 264 265 266

267 268 269 270 271 272 273

274 275 276 277 278 279 280

PLATE 11

No.	Weight		Die axis	Moneyer	Hild. type	Hild. no.	
	Gm.	Gr.					

CRICKLADE (*contd.*)

No.	Gm.	Gr.	Die axis	Moneyer	type	no.	
281	1·11	17·1	↓	ÆLFPINE	G	o[1]	Lübeck find 89.
282	1·17	18·1	→	ÆLGELPINE	G	243	Lübeck find 87 (*sic!*)
283	1·15	17·7	→	—	G	243	Same dies. Bruun 82.
284	1·14	17·6	↑	ÆLINE	H	o	Lübeck find 90.
285	1·14	17·6	←	—	H	o	Same dies. Bruun 83.
286	0·97	14·9	→	ÆLPINE	E	246	Lübeck find 91.
287	1·05	16·3	→	—	E	cf. 246	(CROCI:) Same obv. die as 288 and 289. Kelstrup find 1859.
288	1·15	17·7	←	ÆÐELPINE	E	247	Same dies as 289; same obv. die as 287. Lübeck find 92.
289	1·12	17·3	↖	—	E	247	As last. Bruun 80, ex Bille-Brahe.
290	(1·35)	(20·8)	↑	GO(DE)MAN	E	o[1]	Beskrivelse Tillæg 1794, no. 30, R & D 9. Chipped. Same dies as *BMC*, 43.
291	0·94	14·5	→	GODPINE	E var.	o[2]	Bust to right, with sceptre, Mohr, auction 1847, no. 1751.
292	1·11	17·1	←	—	G	251	R & D XXV. Frost, auction 1827, no. 11.
293	1·27	19·6	↓	HILDRED	E	252[3]	Beskrivelse 1791, no. 21. R & D 10.
294	0·97	14·9	↑	SIDEPINE	Ed	255	Enner find 1849.
295	1·17	18·1	→	TOCA	E	260	Stolpehuse find 1837.
296	1·15	17·7	→	—	E	260	Same dies. Bruun 81.
297	1·17	18·1	←	—	E	o	(CROGLA) Strøyberg 1839.

CRUCERN (CREWKERNE)

No.	Gm.	Gr.	Die axis	Moneyer	type	no.	
298	1·06	16·3	→	BRIHTPII	H	cf. 262	Historisk-antikvarisk Selskab, Aarhus 1890.
299	(0·65)	(10·1)	↓	(PI)NAS	E	cf. 264	Kongsø plantage find 72. Broken and chipped.
300	1·06	16·3	↓	PINAS	E	265	Kelstrup find 1859.
301	1·07	16·5	↓	—	E	265	Same dies. Bruun 84.

DEORABY (DERBY)

No.	Gm.	Gr.	Die axis	Moneyer	type	no.	
302	0·81	12·5	↑	SVERTINC	G	o	Stolpehuse find 1837.
303	1·17	18·1	↑	SPARTINC	G	273	Lyngby find 1861.
304	1·10	16·9	↑	—	G	273	Bruun 85.
305	0·99	15·3	←	SPERTINC	H	276	Same obv. die as 307. Haagerup find 132.
306	0·98	15·1	→	—	H	276	Stockholm 1854.
307	1·01	15·6	↑	—	H	276	Same obv. die as 305. Bruun 86.
308	0·81	12·5	→	—	H	277	Lübeck find 97.

[1] Moneyer not recorded by Hildebrand for the mint in this reign.
[2] Variant not recorded in Hildebrand. Moneyer not recorded for type.
[3] Scandinavian?—see p. ix.

PLATE 11

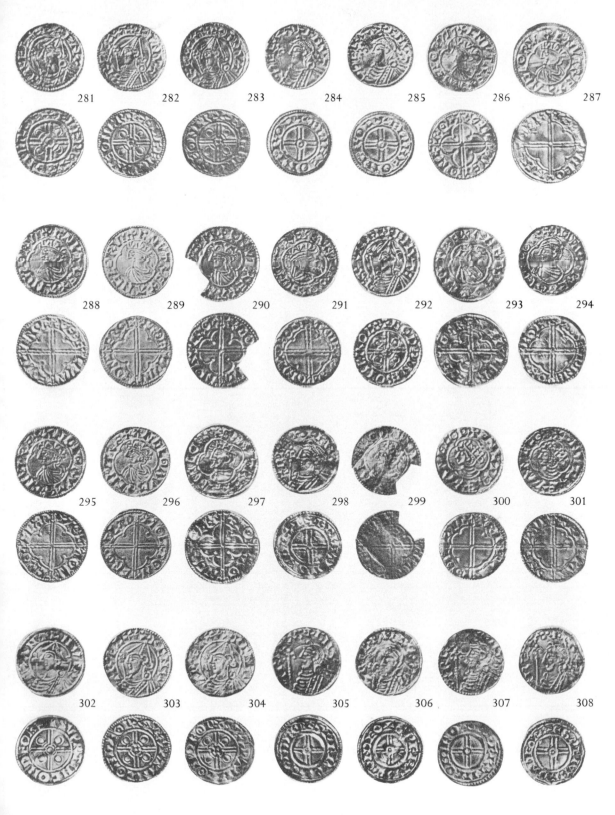

281   282   283   284   285   286   287

288   289   290   291   292   293   294

295   296   297   298   299   300   301

302   303   304   305   306   307   308

PLATE 12

No.	Weight Gm.	Gr.	Die axis	Moneyer	Hild. type	no.	
DERBY (*contd.*)							
309	1·01	15·6	↓	SPERTINC	H	277	Bruun 87.
310	1·09	16·8	→	—	I	278	Gartz, auction 1901, no. 1159.
311	0·90	13·9	↓	ÞVLFAH	I	o[1]	Bergsøe 1877.
				(See also no. 414)			
DOFERAN (DOVER)							
312	0·92	14·2	↑	ÆLFSTAN	H	cf. 285	No provenance.
313	1·08	16·6	←	BOGA	H	286	Munksjørup find 1829.
314	1·07	16·5	↑	—	H	286	Same dies. Bruun 99.
315	0·98	15·1	→	—	H	cf. 286	Same rev. die as 313–14. Schou, auction 1926, no. 14. Broken.
316	1·10	16·9	←	—	H	287	Devegge 1287.
317	1·10	16·9	↑	—	H	287	Same rev. die as 316; same obv. die as 318. Hauberg, auction 1929, no. 120.
318	1·07	16·5	→	—	H	287	Same obv. die as 317. Agerskov 1922.
319	0·83	12·8	→	—	H	287	Same dies as 317. Bruun 100.
320	1·08	16·6	→	—	H	288	Same dies as 318. Bruun 101, ex Bille-Brahe.
321	0·92	14·2	→	—	H	289	No provenance.
322	1·03	15·9	→	—	H	o	(DOFRA) Petersen, auction 1917, no. 75.
323	1·00	15·4	→	—	H	o	(DOR) Lübeck find 150.
324	1·01	15·6	→	—	I	cf. 290	(RECX) Thomsen 9058.
325	(0·76)	(11·7)	↓	—	I	cf. 290	Same dies. Bruun 110. Chipped.
326	1·06	16·3	↑	CINSIGE	G	293	Lübeck find 108.
327	0·88	13·6	←	—	G	294	Same rev. die as 326; same obv. die as 330. Lübeck find 107.
328	0·95	14·6	←	—	G	cf. 294	(AN) Lübeck find 107 var.
329	1·00	15·4	↓	—	G	cf. 294	(DOF) Same obv. die as 339. Lübeck find 103.
330	0·99	15·3	↓	—	G	cf. 294	(DOFRAN) Same obv. die as 327. Enner find 1849.
331	0·90	13·9	→	—	G	cf. 294	(DOF) Lübeck find 102.
332	0·87	13·4	↓	—	G	cf. 294	Same dies. Bruun 89, ex Bille-Brahe.
333	0·98	15·1	↓	—	G	cf. 294	Same rev. die as 331–2. Bruun 90.
334	1·05	16·2	→	—	H	295	Lübeck find 104.
335	1·06	16·3	↑	—	H	295	Same dies. Bruun 102.
336	1·11	17·1	↓	—	H	296	Same dies as 337. Lübeck find 106.

[1] Moneyer not recorded by Hildebrand for the type for Cnut. Recorded for Harthacnut (H. 21).

PLATE 12

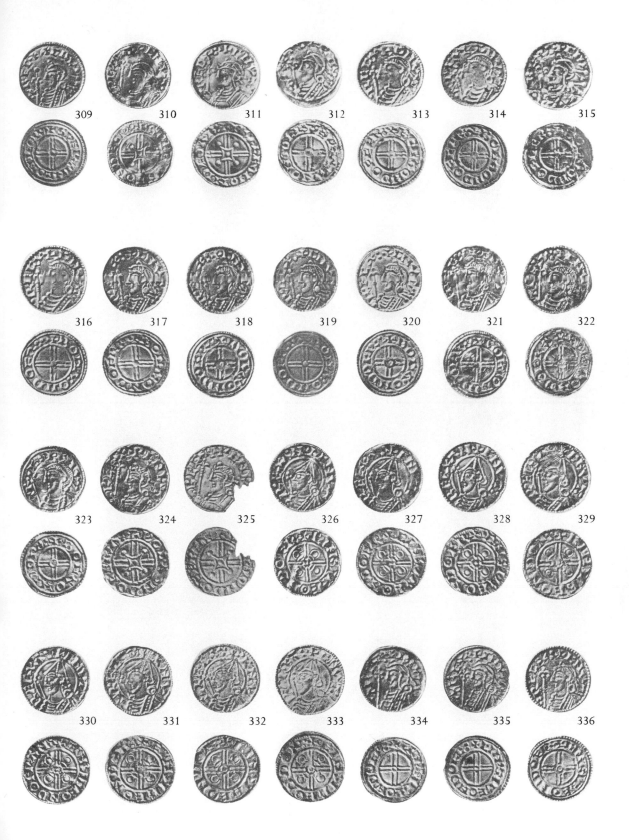

309 310 311 312 313 314 315

316 317 318 319 320 321 322

323 324 325 326 327 328 329

330 331 332 333 334 335 336

PLATE 13

E

No.	Weight Gm.	Gr.	Die axis	Moneyer	type	Hild. no.	
						Hild.	
	Weight		*Die*				
	Gm.	*Gr.*	*axis*	*Moneyer*	*type*	*no.*	

DOVER (*contd.*)

No.	Gm.	Gr.	axis	Moneyer	type	no.	
337	1·11	17·1	↑	CINSIGE	H	296	Same dies as 336. Bruun 103, ex Bille-Brahe.
338	1·06	16·3	→	—	H	cf. 296	Lübeck find 105.
339	0·91	14·1	↓	CINSIGGE	G	cf. 298	(RECXA:) Same obv. die as 329. Bech, auction 1906, no. 57.
340	1·00	15·4	↓	—	G	299	Enegaard find 1862.
341	(0·62)	(9·5)	↓	CINSTAN	H	300	Kongsø plantage find 74. Broken.
342	0·98	15·1	←	EDSIGE	G	307	Lübeck find 110.
343	0·89	13·7	↓	—	G	cf. 307	(RECX) Lübeck find 109.
344	0·90	13·9	↘	—	G	cf. 307	Same dies. Bruun 91, ex Bille-Brahe.
345	0·93	14·3	←	EDSIGEE	G	308	Same rev. die as 346; same dies as 347. Enner find 1849.
346	1·01	15·6	↓	—	G	308	Same rev. die as 345 and 347. Lübeck find 111.
347	1·04	16·1	←	—	G	308	Same rev. die as 346; same dies as 345. Lübeck find 111.
348	(0·49)	(7·5)	↓	(ED)SI	E	0	Hede 1946. Cut halfpenny.
349	0·89	13·7	↑	EDÞII	H	0	Lübeck find 114.
350	1·20	18·5	→	—	H	0	Same dies. Bruun 104, ex Bille-Brahe.
351	0·99	15·3	↑	EDÞINE	H	312	Same obv. die as 353 and 357; same rev. die as 352. Lübeck find 115.
352	1·03	15·9	→	—	H	cf. 312	(REC) Same rev. die as 351. Lübeck find 116.
353	0·99	15·3	→	—	H	314	Same obv. die as 351 and 357. Ernst, donation 1964.
354	1·00	15·4	←	—	H	cf. 314	(RE+) Same rev. die as 355. No provenance.
355	1·06	16·3	↑	—	H	315	Same obv. die as 358 and 361; same rev. die as 354. Bruun 105, ex Bille-Brahe.
356	1·11	17·1	→	—	H	317	Same obv. die as 359 and 360; same rev. die as 358. No provenance.
357	0·92	14·2	↓	—	H	318	Same obv. die as 351 and 353. Lübeck find 122.
358	1·07	16·5	↑	—	H	320	Same obv. die as 355 and 361; same rev. die as 356. No provenance.
359	1·07	16·5	↓	—	H	321	Same obv. die as 356; same dies as 360. Lübeck find 123.
360	1·07	16·5	↑	—	H	321	Same obv. die as 356; same dies as 359. Bruun 106.
361	1·14	17·6	→	—	H	322	Same obv. die as 355 and 358. Lübeck find 125.
362	1·25	19·3	↑	ETSIGE	G	324	Store Valby find 1839 (or Enner find 1849).
363	0·93	14·3	↑	—	G	324	Same dies. Bruun 92.
364	1·10	16·9	↓	—	H	325	Lübeck find 126.

PLATE 13

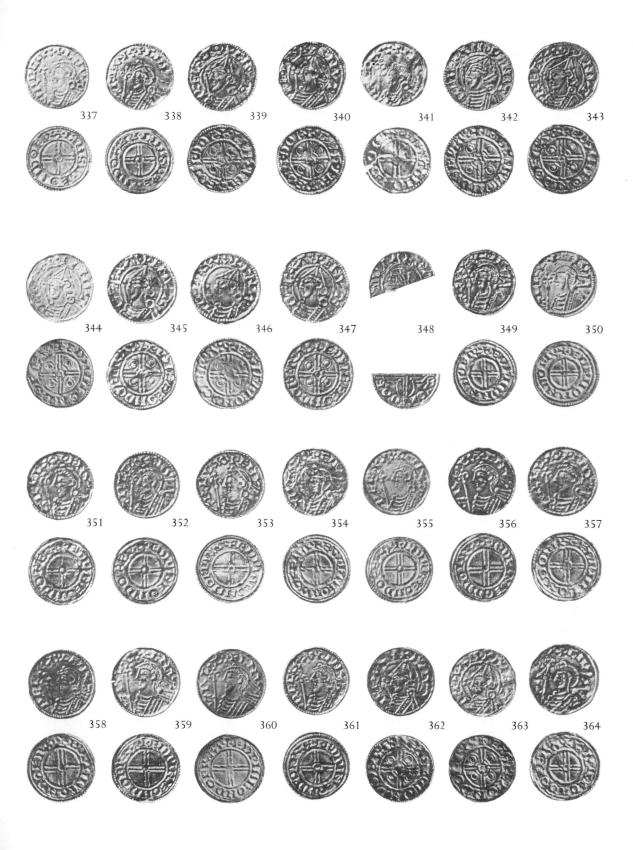

337 338 339 340 341 342 343

344 345 346 347 348 349 350

351 352 353 354 355 356 357

358 359 360 361 362 363 364

PLATE 14

DOVER (*contd.*)

No.	Gm.	Gr.	axis	Moneyer	type	Hild. no.	Notes
365	1·00	15·4	↓	ETSIGE	H	328	Same obv. die as 368–9. Haagerup find 136.
366	0·89	13·7	↑	—	H	cf. 328	(REC) Same obv. die as 370. Haagerup find 137.
367	0·83	12·8	↑	—	H	329	Lübeck find 127.
368	1·11	17·1	←	—	H	329	Same dies as 369; same obv. die as 365; same rev. die as 370. Lübeck find 127.
369	1·05	16·2	←	—	H	330	Same dies as 368; same obv. die as 365; same rev. die as 370. Bruun 107.
370	1·00	15·4	↓	—	H	cf. 330	(REC) Same rev. die as 368–9; same obv. die as 366. Lübeck find 128.
371	1·03	15·9	↓	—	H	cf. 331	(REX/ON) Stolpehuse find 1837.
372	1·11	17·1	↑	—	H	cf. 331	(ON) Lübeck find 131.
373	1·12	17·3	↑	—	H	cf. 331	(ON) Same dies. Bruun 108, ex Bille-Brahe.
374	1·07	16·5	↓	ETSIGEE	K	o[1]	Haagerup find 140. Cracked.
375	1·39	21·4	↑	GODMAN	E	333	Kelstrup find 1859.
376	1·16	17·9	↑	LEOFꝔINE	E	335	Lübeck find (not in *ZfN*).
377	1·03	15·9	←	—	E	335	Same dies. Bruun 88.
378	0·95	14·6	↓	—	E	cf. 335	(ANGLORVMO) Cross of 4 pellets behind bust; rev., single pellets in field outside quatrefoil. Mohr, auction 1847, no. 1752.
379	0·90	13·9	↑	—	G	337	Lübeck find 132.
380	0·97	14·9	←	—	G	337	Same rev. die as 381 and 383. Kongsø plantage find 75.
381	0·92	14·2	→	—	G	cf. 337	(AN) Same obv die as 382; same rev. die as 380 and 383. Lübeck find 133.
382	0·91	14·1	↖	—	G	cf. 337	Same obv. die as 381. Bruun 93.
383	0·96	14·8	→	—	G	o	Same rev. die as 380–1. Bruun 94, ex Bille-Brahe.
384	0·92	14·2	↑	—	G	338	Lübeck find 140.
385	1·13	17·4	→	—	H	339	Same rev. die as 386. Lübeck find 134.
386	1·09	16·8	←	—	H	339	Same rev. die as 385. Beskrivelse, Tillæg 1794 no. 17. R & D 11.
387	0·92	14·2	↓	—	H	339	Kirchhoff 1916.
388	1·09	16·8	↓	—	H	cf. 342	(DOFER) Same rev. die as 389. Lübeck find 137.
389	1·06	16·3	↓	—	H	cf. 342	Same obv. die as 390 and 392; same rev. die as 388. Lübeck find 137.
390	1·05	16·2	←	—	H	cf. 342	(DOFR) Same obv. die as 389, same rev. die as 391 and same dies as 392. Lübeck find 139.
391	1·10	16·9	←	—	H	cf. 342	(DOFR) (REX). Same rev. die as 390 and 392. Enner find 1849.
392	1·11	17·1	←	—	H	cf. 342	(DOFR) Same dies as 390; same obv. die as 389; same rev. die as 391; Bruun 109.

[1] Moneyer not recorded by Hildebrand for the type for Cnut.

PLATE 14

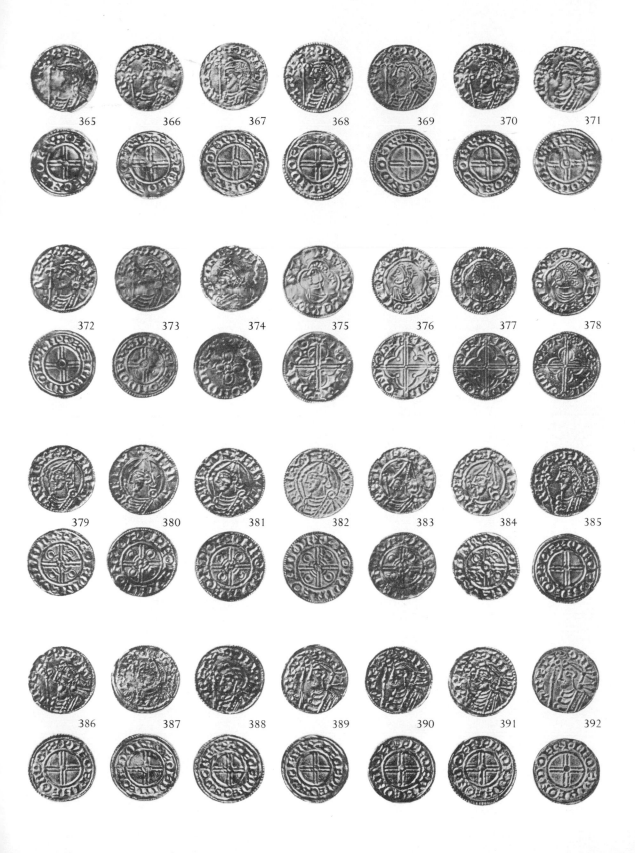

PLATE 15

No.	Weight Gm.	Gr.	Die axis	Moneyer	Hild. type	no.	
DOVER (*contd.*)							
393	1·16	17·9	→	LEOFPINE	K	343	Bonderup find 1854.
394	1·10	16·9	←	LIOFPINE	E	o	Benzon, donation 1885, no. 4.
395	1·00	15·4	↓	LVFEPINE	G	o	Same dies as 396; same obv. die as 401. R & D XXVII. Timm, auction 1831, no. 5.
396	0·97	14·9	←	—	G	o	Same dies as 395; same obv. die as 401. Bruun 95.
397	0·99	15·3	↑	LVFPINE	G	344	Same rev. die as 400. Lübeck find 144.
398	1·03	15·9	→	—	G	cf. 344	(—A) Lübeck find 145.
399	1·02	15·7	↑	—	G	cf. 344	(—A) Same dies. Bruun 96, ex Bille-Brahe.
400	0·95	14·6	→	—	G	cf. 344	(—AN) Same rev. die as 397. Lübeck find 146.
401	1·04	16·1	→	—	G	346	Same obv. die as 395–6. Lyngby find 1861.
402	1·08	16·6	↑	—	G	347	Thomsen 9061.
403	0·97	14·9	↑	—	G	347	Same dies. Bruun 97.
404	0·87	13·4	→	—	G	o	(DOFRI) Store Valby find 1839. Broken.
405	1·12	17·3	↑	MANINC	Ei	349	Kelstrup find 1859. Broken.
406	1·17	18·1	→	SPEARTAFE	G	350	Kelstrup find 1859.
407	1·08	16·6	↓	—	G	350	Same dies. Bruun 98.
408	1·05	16·2	↑	SPERTAFE	G	351	Lübeck find 149.
DORCEASTER (DORCHESTER)							
409	1·06	16·3	↓	HPATEMAN	I	353	Bolbygaard find 1872.
410	1·18	18·2	←	SPET	G	357	Kelstrup find 1859.
411	0·96	14·8	↓	—	G	357	Same dies. Bruun 111, ex Bille-Brahe, ex Siökrona 1883.
412	1·25	19·3	←	SPETA	H	360	Bonderup find 1854.
413	1·11	17·1	↑	—	H	360	Same dies. Bruun 112.
414	1·10	16·9	↑	PVLFSIGE	E	o[1]	Kelstrup find 1859.
EANBYRH (?)							
415	1·32	20·3	↙	SPET	E	cf. 118	Bruun 38.
EAXECEASTER (EXETER)							
416	1·13	17·4	→	ÆFICC	H	362	Store Valby find 1839.
417	1·13	17·4	←	—	H	362	Same dies. Bruun 125.
418	0·87	13·4	↓	ÆLFSTAN	G	o[2]	(MOEAXCA) Bruun 117.
419	1·05	16·2	↓	ÆLFPINE	G	363	No provenance.
420	1·02	15·7	←	—	G	363	Same dies as 421; same obv. die as 422. Bonderup find 1854.

[1] Stylistically this coin seems more likely to be of Derby where the spelling DOR is occasionally found. Moneyer not recorded by Hildebrand for either mint in this reign.

[2] Moneyer not recorded by Hildebrand for the type. The form of obverse legend (Hild. a3, ir. 33) and the copulative MO are unprecedented on a West Country coin of this type.

PLATE 15

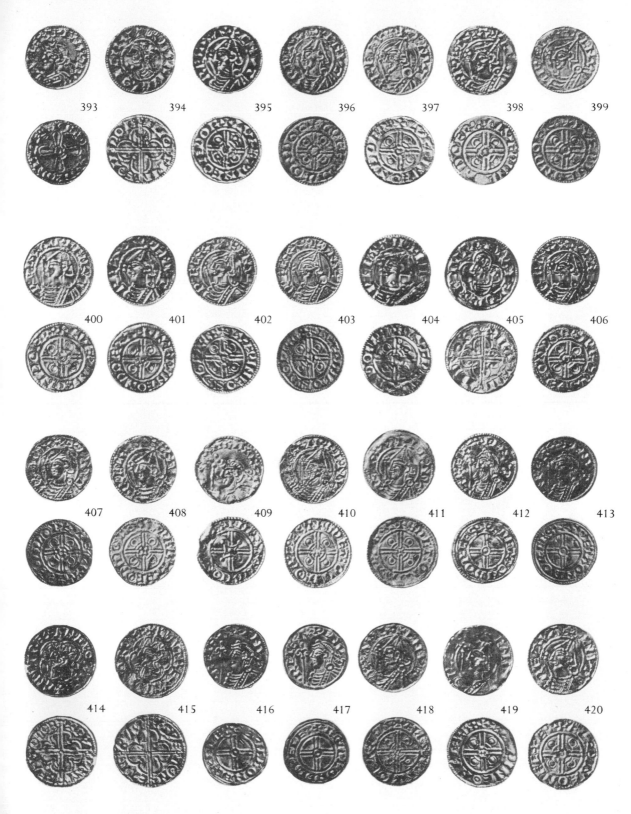

393 394 395 396 397 398 399

400 401 402 403 404 405 406

407 408 409 410 411 412 413

414 415 416 417 418 419 420

PLATE 16

No.	Weight Gm.	Gr.	Die axis	Moneyer	Hild. type	no.	
EXETER (contd.)							
421	1·00	15·4	↓	ÆLFÞINE	G	363	Same dies as 420; same obv. die as 422. Bruun 118.
422	1·05	16·2	→	—	G	cf. 363	(EEX:) Same obv. die as 420–1. Siökrona 1883.
423	1·15	17·7	→	—	H	364	No provenance.
424	1·02	15·7	→	—	H	364	Same dies. Bruun 126, ex Bille-Brahe.
425	1·14	17·6	↑	—	H	366	Lübeck find 154.
426	0·88	13·6	→	CARLA	E	cf. 367	(EAXC) Bech, auction 1906, no. 64.
427	0·75	11·5	↘	—	E	cf. 367	(EAXC) Same dies. Bruun 113.
428	1·05	16·2	↑	—	E	367	Kelstrup find 1859.
429	0·67	10·3	→	CARLAA	Ed	370	Kelstrup find 1859.
430	0·99	15·3	←	DODDA	G	0[1]	Enner find 1849.
431	0·99	15·3	↓	EADMÆR	E	0[1]	Kelstrup find 1859.
3259	0·98	15·1	↓	—	E	0	Hess, auction 1891, no. 1039. (Plate 117.)
432	1·11	17·1	→	EALDEBERD	G	375	R & D XXX. Frost, auction 1827, no. 13.
433	1·07	16·5	↑	—	G	375	Same dies. Bruun 119, ex Bille-Brahe.
434	1·13	17·4	←	—	G	cf. 375	(ANG) Purchased 1842.
435	1·10	16·9	↓	—	G	cf. 375	(ANG) Same dies. Bruun 120.
436	1·13	17·4	↓	EDMÆR	G	376	Enner find 1849.
437	1·12	17·3	→	—	G	376	Same dies. Bruun 121.
438	1·14	17·6	↑	—	G	377	Store Valby find 1839.
439	1·13	17·4	↓	—	G	377	Same dies. Bruun 122.
440	0·94	14·5	←	EDSIE	G	cf. 378	(—A) R & D XXXI. Timm, auction 1831 no. 6.
441	(0·82)	(12·6)	→	EDSIGE	E	0[1]	Ahlander, donation 1851. Chipped.
442	0·92	14·2	↓	—	E	0[1]	Same dies. Ernst donation 1964, ex Hauberg, auction 1929 no. 126.
443	1·09	16·8	↓	—	G	381	Store Valby find 1839.
444	1·13	17·4	↓	—	G	381	Same dies. Bruun 123, ex Bille-Brahe.
445	1·08	16·6	→	EDÞINE	H	384	Lübeck find 160.
446	1·14	17·6	↑	—	H	385	Same dies as 448; same obv. die as 447. R & D 12.
447	1·04	16·1		—	H	385	Same obv. die as 446 and 448. Haagerup find 142.
448	1·11	17·1	↑	—	H	385	Same dies as 446; same obv. die as 447. Bruun 127.

[1] Moneyer not recorded by Hildebrand for the type.

PLATE 16

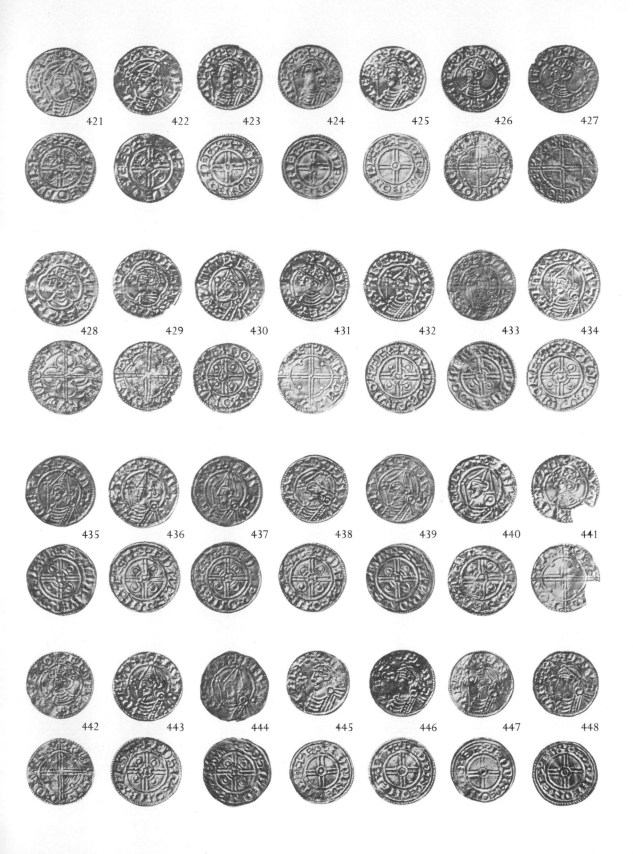

421 422 423 424 425 426 427

428 429 430 431 432 433 434

435 436 437 438 439 440 441

442 443 444 445 446 447 448

PLATE 17

F

No.	Weight Gm.	Gr.	Die axis	Moneyer	Hild. type	no.	
EXETER (*contd.*)							
449	1·15	17·7	↓	ETSIGE	G	387	Enner find 1849.
450	1·11	17·1	↑	GOD	E	cf. 389	(ANGLORV) Same dies as 452. Bruun 114, ex Bille-Brahe.
451	0·97	14·9	↑	—	E	390	Enner find 1849.
452	1·05	16·2	↓	—	E	cf. 389	(ANGLORV) Same dies as 450. Enner find 1849.
453	0·79	12·2	↑	—	E	o	Haagerup find 143.
454	1·04	16·1	←	—	E	o	Same dies. Bruun 115.
455	1·15	17·8	↑	GODBRYT	G	o¹	Siökrona 1883.
456	1·10	16·9	↑	GODD	G	cf. 392	(ANG:) Benzon, donation 1885, no. 6.
457	1·15	17·8	↓	—	G	cf. 392	Same rev. die as 458. (AN) Lübeck find 162.
458	1·14	17·6	↓	—	G	393	Same obv. die as 457. Purchased 1879.
459	1·15	17·8	←	GODÞINE	E	o²	s before head. Enner find 1849.
460	1·15	17·8	↓	HVNEMAN	H	394	Stockholm 1885.
461	1·30	20·1	↓	HVNEÞINE	E	cf. 396	(OEX) Lübeck find 165.
462	0·80	12·3	↓	HVNNI	H	o³	Lübeck find 163.
463	0·97	14·9	←	ISEGOD	E	cf. 397	(EAXCE) Bolbygaard 1872.
464	1·12	17·3	↓	—	E	398	R & D XXXIII. Thomsen 9070.
465	1·07	16·5	↓	—	E	398	Same dies. Bruun 116, ex Bille-Brahe, ex Munk-sjørup find 1829.
466	1·03	15·9	←	LEOFÞINE	G	400	Lübeck find 166.
467	0·93	14·3	←	—	G	401	Store Valby find 1839.
468	0·83	12·8	→	MANA	G	o⁴	Enner find 1849.
469	0·88	13·6	↓	MANAN	G	o⁴	Lübeck find 167.
470	1·17	18·1	↓	MANNA	E	404	Kelstrup find 1859.
471	1·00	15·4	→	—	E	405	Lübeck find 167a.
472	0·96	14·8	↓	—	E	406	Haagerup find 144.
473	0·90	13·9	↓	SÆÞINE	G	409	Petersen, auction 1917, no. 79.
474	1·10	16·9	←	—	G	cf. 411	Same obv. die as 475–6. Store Valby find 1839.
475	1·15	17·7	↓	—	G	411	(ECCXCE:) Same dies as 476; same obv. die as 474. Bruun 124, ex Bille-Brahe.
476	1·13	17·4	←	—	G	cf. 411	Same dies as 475; same obv. die as 474. Store Valby find 1839.

¹ Personal name otherwise apparently unrecorded in the Anglo-Saxon series.
² Moneyer not recorded by Hildebrand for mint in this reign.
³ Though previously identified as Exeter, this seems more likely to be Malmesbury.
⁴ Moneyer not recorded by Hildebrand for the type.

PLATE 17

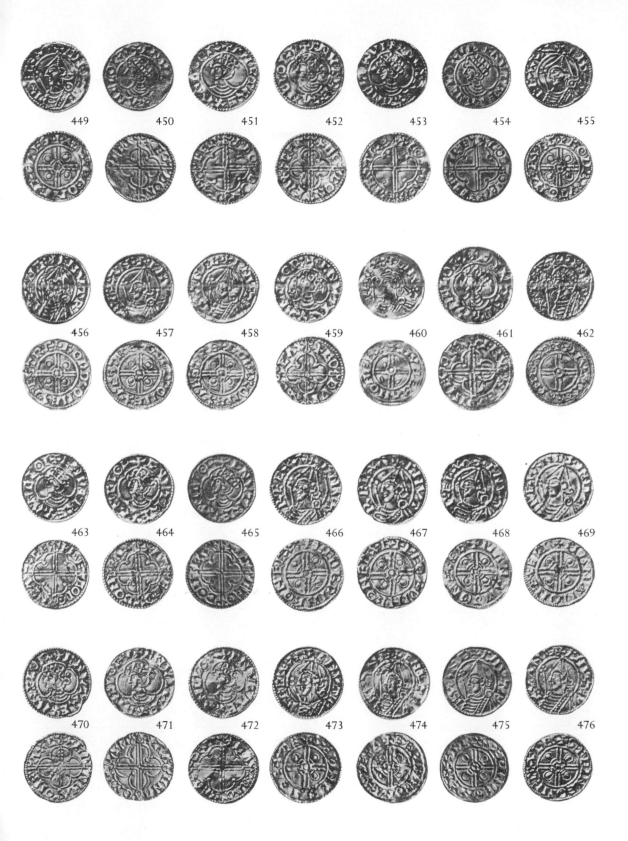

449 450 451 452 453 454 455

456 457 458 459 460 461 462

463 464 465 466 467 468 469

470 471 472 473 474 475 476

PLATE 18

No.	Weight Gm.	Gr.	Die axis	Moneyer	type	Hild. no.	
EXETER (*contd.*)							
477	1·04	16·1	←	SCVLA	G	cf. 412	(ECXEC:) Lübeck find 169.
478	1·10	16·9	↑	—	H	414	Siökrona 1883.
479	1·14	17·6	↑	ÐEGENÞINE	H	cf. 415	Lübeck find 155.
480	1·14	17·6	←	ÐEGNÞINE	H	415	Same obv. die. Lyngby find 1861.
481	1·17	18·1	↑	—	H	416	Bruun 128.
482	1·15	17·7	↑	—	H	416 var.	Same obv. die. Bruun 129.
483	(0·60)	(9·3)	←	ÐVRGOD	E	o[1]	Thomsen 9071. Chipped.
484	0·91	14·1	↑	—	E	o[1]	Hess, auction 1891, no. 912.
485	0·80	12·3	←	ÞINE	E	cf. 417	(EAXCE) Bech, auction 1906, no. 67.
486	1·44	22·2	←	ÞVLFME	E	o[2]	Haagerup find 145.
487	0·97	14·9	→	ÞVLFSTAN	E	421	Enner find 1849.
488	1·06	16·3	↑	ÞVLFÞERD	G	cf. 426	(AN) Lübeck find 170.
489	1·04	16·1	→	ÞVLSTAN	G	427	Lübeck find 172.
490	1·04	16·1	→	—	G	428	Lübeck find 173.
491	1·06	16·4	→	—	G	o	Kelstrup find 1859.
492	1·06	16·4	←	—	G	o	(EVCX) Lübeck find 174.
493	1·14	17·6	↑	—	H	430	Lübeck find 171.
494	1·10	16·10	↑	—	H	430	Same dies. Bruun 130, ex Bille-Brahe.
EOFERÞIC (YORK)							
495	1·04	16·1	→	ÆELÞINE	H	431	Lübeck find 175.
496	1·07	16·5	←	ÆGELÞINE	H	433	Thomsen 9072.
497	1·07	16·5	↓	—	H	433	Same dies. Bruun 202.
498	1·08	16·6	→	—	H	433	Same rev. die as 499. Haagerup find 146.
499	1·03	15·9	←	—	H	433	Same obv. die as 500, 502–3; same rev. die as 498. Lübeck find 176.
500	1·14	17·6	←	—	H	437	Same obv. die as 499, 502–3; same rev. die as 501. Lübeck find 178.
501	1·10	16·9	↓	—	H	437	Same rev. die as 500. Lübeck find 178.
502	1·15	17·7	↑	—	H	437	Same dies as 503; same obv. die as 499-500. Haagerup find 147.
503	1·17	18·1	↑	—	H	438	Same dies as 502; same obv. die as 499–500. Bruun 203, ex Bille-Brahe.
504	1·10	16·9	↑	—	I	439	Haagerup find 148.

[1] Moneyer not recorded by Hildebrand for the mint in this reign (but cf. *BMC* 59).

[2] Moneyer not recorded by Hildebrand for the mint in this reign, but the name Wulfmær is found in this type at Gothaburh. Coins of this mint sometimes die-link with Exeter.

PLATE 18

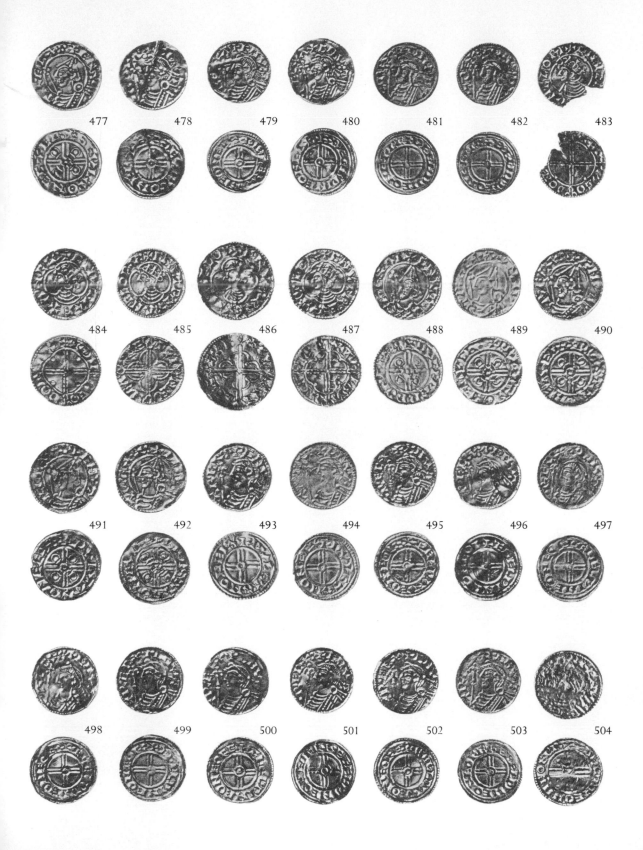

477   478   479   480   481   482   483

484   485   486   487   488   489   490

491   492   493   494   495   496   497

498   499   500   501   502   503   504

PLATE 19

No.	Weight Gm.	Gr.	Die axis	Moneyer	type	Hild. no.	
YORK (contd.)							
505	1·14	17·6	↓	ÆLFERE	I	441	Munksjørup find 1829.
506	1·18	18·2	←	—	I	441	Same dies. Bruun 232.
507	1·16	17·9	←	—	I	441 var.	Lassen.
508	0·97	14·9	←	ÆÐELÞINE	G	442	Lübeck find 180.
509	1·01	15·6	↘	—	G	442	Bruun 161, ex Bille-Brahe.
510	0·97	14·9	←	—	G	442	Same dies. Stolpehuse find 1837.
511	0·96	14·8	→	—	G	442 var.	Ernst, donation 1964, ex Hauberg, auction 1929, no. 150.
512	1·00	15·4	↓	—	G	cf. 444	(AN) Schou, auction 1926, no. 17.
513	1·00	15·4	↑	—	G	444	Enner find 1849.
514	1·01	15·6	↖	—	G	444	Same dies. Bruun 162.
515	0·97	14·9	↓	ÆDLÞIN	G	o	Lübeck find 179.
516	1·06	16·4	↓	ALFSTAN	G	o[1]	Enner find 1849.
517	0·86	13·2	↓	ARCIL	H	o	Gartz, auction 1901, no. 1163.
518	1·19	18·3	→	ARCITELL	I	448	Bonderup find 1854.
519	1·11	17·1	↙	—	I	449	Haagerup find 150.
520	1·12	17·3	↓	—	I	449	Same dies. Bruun 233. Pierced.
521	0·97	14·9	↘	ARNCETEL	E	451	Thomsen 9074.
522	1·07	16·5	↓	—	E	452	Same obv. die. Enner find 1849.
523	1·00	15·4	→	—	E	452 var.	Bruun 132, ex Bille-Brahe.
619	1·04	16·1	→	—	E	cf. 452 var.	Beskrivelse, Tillæg 1794, p. 19, no. 5. R & D 16. (Plate 23.)
524	1·14	17·6	→	—	G	456	Same dies as 525; same obv. die as 526. Lübeck find 181.
525	1·15	17·7	→	—	G	456	Same dies as 524; same obv. die as 526. Bruun 163.
526	1·04	16·1	↓	—	G	457	Same obv. die as 524–5. Bruun 164, ex Bille-Brahe.
527	1·10	16·9	↑	ARNCETL	G	458	Enner find 1849.
528	0·97	14·9	→	ARNCYTEL	H	461	Sanct Jørgensbjerg find 6.
529	1·17	18·1	↑	ARNGRIM	I	o (cf. 559)	Bonderup find 1854.
530	0·99	15·3	↑	ASCVTR	E	463	Lübeck find 182.
531	0·91	14·1	↑	ASGOD	G	cf. 467	(AN) Enner find 1849.
532	0·95	14·6	↑	ASGOVT	G	470	Store Valby find 1839.

[1] Moneyer not recorded by Hildebrand for the type.

PLATE 19

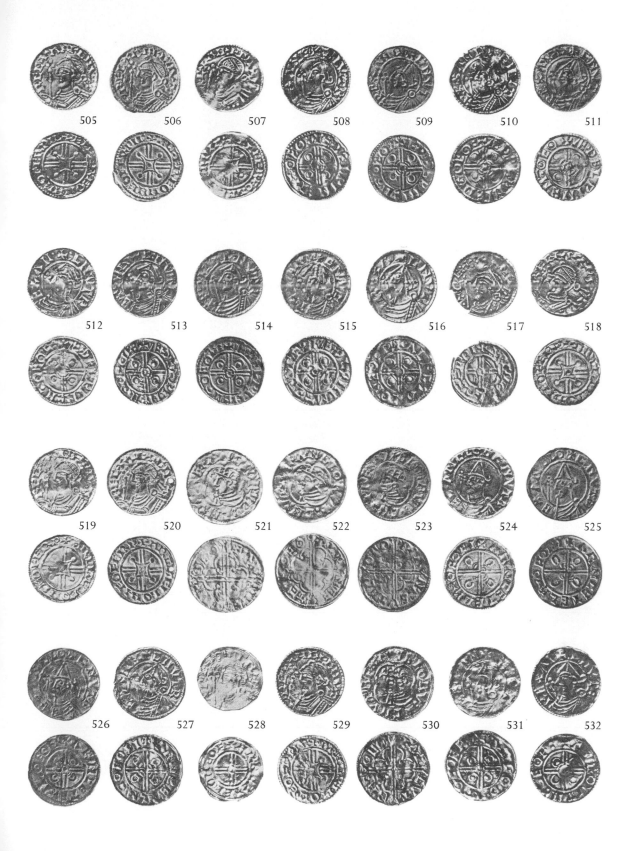

505   506   507   508   509   510   511

512   513   514   515   516   517   518

519   520   521   522   523   524   525

526   527   528   529   530   531   532

PLATE 20

No.	Weight Gm.	Gr.	Die axis	Moneyer	Hild. type	no.	
YORK (contd.)							
533	0·95	14·6	←	ASGOVT	G	471	Thomsen 9075.
534	1·00	15·4	→	—	G	472	Stockholm 1856.
535	0·94	14·5	↖	—	G	472	Same dies. Bruun 165.
536	1·09	16·8	↑	—	G	473	Bruun 166, ex Bille-Brahe, ex Stockholm 1854.
537	1·01	15·6	↙	—	G	cf. 473	Ernst, donation 1964, ex Hauberg, auction 1929, no. 152.
538	1·00	15·4	→	—	G	474	Lübeck find 183.
539	1·03	15·9	→	ASGVT	E	cf. 476	(ANGLORI) Bruun 133. Broken.
540	1·29	19·9	←	—	E	477	R & D XXXVII. Timm, auction 1831, no. 7.
541	1·27	19·6	↓	—	E	477	Same dies. Bruun 134, ex Bille-Brahe.
542	1·16	17·9	→	ASGVVT	G	cf. 478	Bonderup find 1854.
543	1·05	16·2	→	BEORN	H	479	Benzon, donation 1885, no. 7.
544	1·01	15·6	↓	—	H	482	No provenance.
545	1·15	17·7	↗	—	H	482	Bruun 205.
546	0·96	14·8	↙	—	H	482	Same dies. Hauberg, auction 1929, no. 171.
547	1·10	16·9	↖	—	H	482	Bruun 204, ex Bille-Brahe.
548	1·19	18·3	↑	—	I	487	R & D Tillæg T. I 13c.
549	1·06	16·3	←	—	I	487	Same dies. Bruun 234.
550	0·99	15·3	→	BIREHTNO	E	488	Lübeck find 190.
551	0·95	14·6	↓	BIRHTNOÐ	E	489	Gartz, auction 1901, no. 1164.
552	0·98	15·1	↓	BREHTNO	E	492	Enner find 1849.
553	0·96	14·8	↓	—	E	492	Same dies. Bruun 135.
554	0·97	14·9	↓	BREHTNOÐ	E	cf. 493	(ANGLORVM) Bech, auction 1906, no. 73.
555	1·03	15·9	↑	—	G	cf. 494	(ANGLOR) Enner find 1849.
556	1·12	17·3	↑	—	G	495	Lübeck find 191.
557	1·10	16·9	↑	—	E, rev. Æthelræd type E, Hild. 644.[1] Bruun 131.			
558	1·05	16·2	↗	BRETECOL	E	497	Hauberg, auction 1929, no. 136. Broken.
559	(1·11)	(17·1)	←	—	E	497	Beskrivelse, Tillæg 1794 p. 11, no. 58, ex Suhm, auction 1802, no. 914. R & D 14. Chipped.
560	1·07	16·5	↑	—	E	cf. 497	(MO) Store Valby find 1839.

[1] Scandinavian?—see p. ix.

PLATE 20

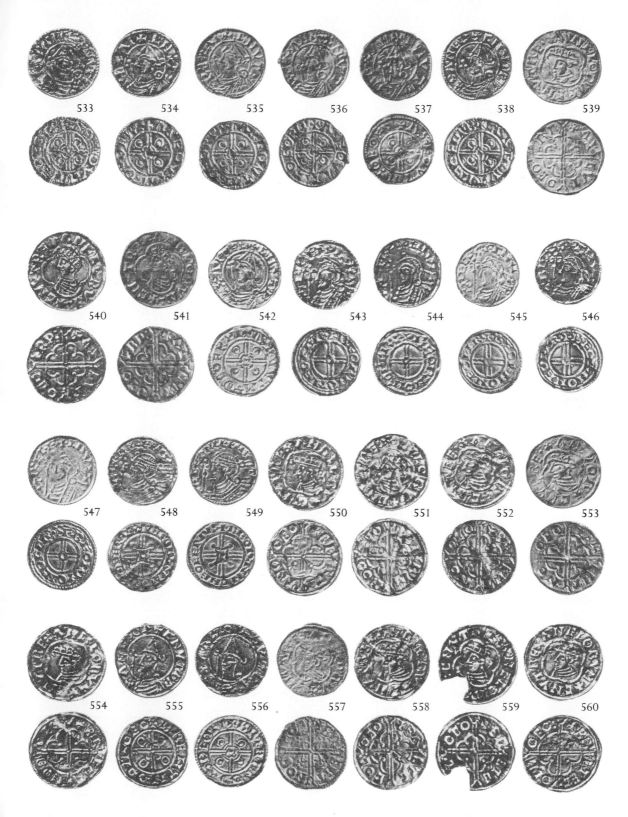

533 534 535 536 537 538 539

540 541 542 543 544 545 546

547 548 549 550 551 552 553

554 555 556 557 558 559 560

PLATE 21

No.	Weight Gm.	Gr.	Die axis	Moneyer	type	Hild. no.	
YORK (contd.)							
561	1·06	16·3	↑	BRETECOL	E	cf. 497	(ANGLORVM) Bruun 136, ex Bille-Brahe.
562	1·08	16·6	↑	BRIHNOÐ	G	o	Moller, Edinburgh 1925.
563	1·11	17·1	↗	BRIHTNOÐ	G	o	Lübeck find 192.
564	1·04	16·1	↓	CETEL	E	503	Kelstrup find 1859.
565	1·19	18·3	↑	—	E	cf. 504	(ANGLOI:) Gartz, auction 1901, no. 1165.
566	1·45	22·4	→	—	E	505	Stolpehuse find 1837.
567	1·26	19·4	←	—	E	505	Same dies. Kelstrup find 1859.
568	0·99	15·3	←	—	E	cf. 506 (a 7)	Enner find 1849.
569	1·08	16·6	↖	—	G	509	Same obv. die as 571; same rev. die as 570. Bruun 167, ex Bille-Brahe.
570	1·10	16·9	←	—	G	cf. 509	(ANG) Same rev. die as 569. Kelstrup find 1859.
571	1·00	15·4	↓	—	G	510	Same obv. die as 569. Kirchhoff 1916.
572	0·96	14·8	↓	—	G	511	Store Valby find 1839.
573	1·08	16·6	←	—	G	513	Same dies as 575; same rev. die as 574. Lübeck find 194.
574	1·01	15·6	←	—	G	513	Same rev. die as 573 and 575. Benzon, donation 1885, no. 8.
575	1·10	16·9	←	—	G	513	Same dies as 573: same rev. die as 574. Enner find 1849.
576	0·90	13·9	↑	CETELL	E	o	Bruun 137, ex Bille-Brahe.
577	0·99	15·3	↖	COLGRIM	E	517	Lübeck find 195.
578	0.95	14·6	↑	—	E	cf. 517	(ANGLOV). Same rev. die. Gartz, auction 1901, no. 1166.
579	1·01	15·6	←	—	E	519	Beskrivelse 1791, no. 27, R & D 15.
580	1·04	16·1	←	—	E	519	Lübeck find 196.
581	1·05	16·2	↘	—	E	519	Same obv. die. Bruun 138, ex Bille-Brahe, ex Thomsen 9078.
582	1·06	16·3	↙	—	E	521	Lübeck find 197.
583	1·06	16·3	→	—	E	523	Store Valby find 1839.
584	1·10	16·9	↑	—	H	527	Hauberg, auction 1929, no. 172.
585	1·12	17·3	→	CRINAN	G	530	Store Valby find 1839.
586	1·08	16·6	←	—	G	o	(EOFRI) Siökrona 1883.
587	0·82	12·7	←	—	G	cf. 531	(ANG) Lübeck find 241.
588	1·03	15·9	←	—	G	534	Ernst, donation 1964, ex Glückstadt, auction 1924, no. 175.

PLATE 21

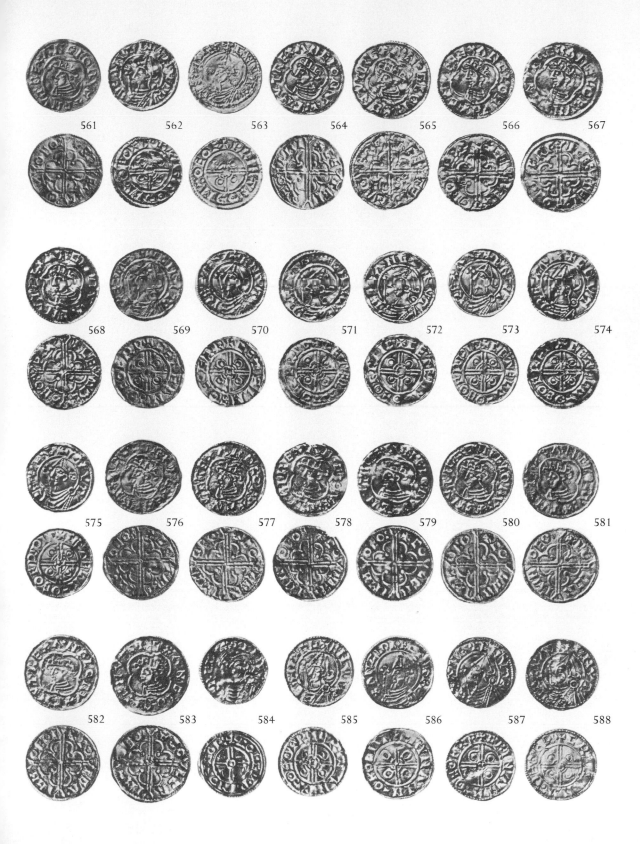

561   562   563   564   565   566   567

568   569   570   571   572   573   574

575   576   577   578   579   580   581

582   583   584   585   586   587   588

PLATE 22

No.	Weight Gm.	Weight Gr.	Die axis	Moneyer	type	Hild. no.	
YORK (contd.)							
589	(0·83)	(12·8)	←	CRVCAN	G	cf. 535 (a 5)	Store Frigaard find 1928. Chipped.
590	1·07	16·5	↑	—	H	536	Lübeck find 198.
591	0·92	14·2	↓	—	H	536	Same rev. die. Lübeck find 199.
592	1·01	15·6	↑	—	H	537	Munksjørup find 1829.
593	0·94	14·5	↖	—	H	cf. 537 (a)	Kongsø plantage find 76, (CN): Bruun 206.
594	0·90	13·9	←	—	H	cf. 538	
595	1·09	16·8	↙	—	H	539	Same dies as 597; same obv. die as 596. Beskrivelse, Tillæg 1794, p. 11, no. 56, ex Suhm, auction 1802, no. 912. R & D XXXVIII. Schubart, auction 1831, no. 2.
596	1·06	16·4	↗	—	H	539	Same obv. die as 593 and 597. Bruun 207, ex Bille-Brahe.
597	1·05	16·2	↗	—	H	539	Same obv. die as 595–6. Louns find 1870, exchanged for Thomsen 9080.
598	1·12	17·3	←	—	H	543	Ernst donation 1964, ex Glückstadt, auction 1924, no. 176.
599	1·02	15·7	→	—	H	543	Same dies. Bruun 208, ex Bille-Brahe.
600	1·10	16·9	↖	—	H	cf. 543	(CNVTT) Bruun 209.
601	1·10	16·9	↗	—	H	cf. 543	(CNVTT) Same dies. Louns find 1870.
602	1·07	16·5	↓	—	H	545	Kongsø plantage find 77.
603	1·03	15·9	→	—	H	546	Store Valby find 1839.
604	1·08	16·6	↑	—	H	o (cf. 539)	(EOFER) Thomsen 9079.
605	1·05	16·2	→	DAHFIN	E	551	Lübeck find 207.
606	1·18	18·2	↑	EARNGRIM	H	553	Same rev. die as 607–8. Lübeck find 208.
607	1·12	17·3	↙	—	H	554	Same dies as 608; same obv. as 609; same rev. die as 606. Lübeck find 209.
608	1·10	16·9	↑	—	H	cf. 554	(REECX) Same dies as 607; same obv. die as 609; same rev. die as 606. Bruun 210.
609	1·15	17·7	→	—	H	555	Same obv. die as 607–8. Haagerup find 154.
610	1·10	16·9	↑	ELFSTAN	E	556	Same dies as 611; same obv. die as 612. Kelstrup find 1859.
611	1·08	16·6	↑	—	E	556	Same dies as 610; same obv. die as 612. Bruun 139, ex Bille-Brahe.
612	1·01	15·6	→	—	E	557	Same obv. die as 610–11. Stockholm 1854.
613	1·41	21·7	↑	—	E	558	Thomsen 9081.
614	1·12	17·3	↑	FÆRÐEIN	H	562	Same dies as 615; same obv. die as 616–17. R & D XL, Thomsen (another specimen: 9082).
615	1·08	16·6	↗	—	H	562	Same dies as 614; same obv. die as 616–17. Bruun 211.
616	1·07	16·5	↓	—	H	563	Same dies as 617; same obv. die as 614–15. Bonderup find 1854.

PLATE 22

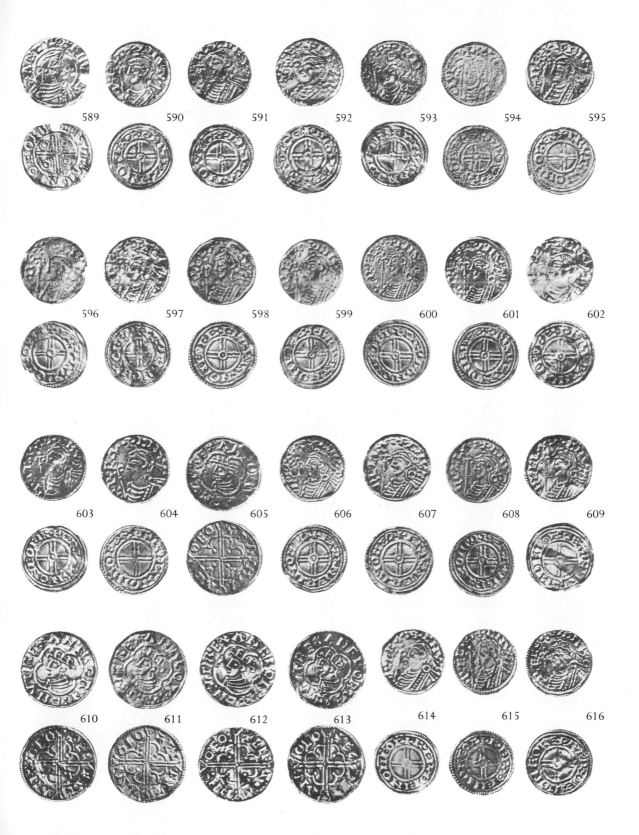

589   590   591   592   593   594   595

596   597   598   599   600   601   602

603   604   605   606   607   608   609

610   611   612   613   614   615   616

PLATE 23

No.	Weight Gm.	Gr.	Die axis	Moneyer	Hild. type	no.	
YORK (contd.)							
617	1·12	17·3	↓	FÆRÐEIN	H	563	Same dies as 616; same obv. die as 615–16. Bruun 212, ex Bille-Brahe.
618	0·98	15·1	→	FÆRÐEN	H	cf. 564	Same obv. die as 639. Moller, Edinburgh 1925.
619							See plate 19.
620	0·85	13·1	↗	FARCRIM	E	cf. 565	Lübeck find 213.
621	1·00	15·4	↙	FARGRIM	E	566	Enner find 1849.
622	0·82	12·6	↗	—	G	o	(EOF:) Store Valby find 1839.
623	1·06	16·3	↙	—	G	568	Same obv. die as 629. Enner find 1849.
624	0·95	14·6	↘	—	G	569	Bruun 168, ex Bille-Brahe. Pierced.
625	1·11	17·1	↙	—	G	cf. 570 (a 5)	Benzon, donation 1885, no. 9.
626	0·98	15·1	↗	—	G	571	Store Valby find 1839.
627	0·98	15·1	↗	—	G	571	Same dies. Enner find 1849.
628	1·00	15·4	←	—	G	572	Lübeck find 216.
629	1·10	16·9	←	—	G	574	Same obv. die as 623; same rev. die as 630–1. Kelstrup find 1859.
630	1·05	16·2	←	—	G	cf. 574 (a 4)	Same dies as 631; same rev. die as 629. Lübeck find 217.
631	1·03	15·9	↙	—	G	cf. 574 (a 4)	Same dies as 630; same rev. die as 629. Bruun 169.
632	0·99	15·3	↖	FARGRM	G	cf. 575	(EOFERÞ) No provenance.
633	1·00	15·4	→	—	G	575	No provenance.
634	1·03	15·9	↙	—	G	575	Same rev. die. Stockholm 1861.
635	1·10	16·9	↘	FARÐEIN	G	577	Beskrivelse, Tillæg 1794, p. 9, no. 4. R & D 17.
636	1·12	17·3	→	—	G	577	Same dies. Bruun 170.
637	1·16	17·9	↓	—	H	578	Lübeck find 219.
638	1·10	16·9	↑	—	H	579	Same rev die. Bruun 213.
639	1·11	17·1	↑	—	H	580	Same obv. die as 618. Gartz, auction 1901, no. 1167.
640	1·04	16·1	→	FARÐIN	G	581	Store Valby find 1839.
641	1·00	15·4	↓	FRETETCOL	E	o	Lübeck find 220.
642	1·04	16·1	↑	FRIÐCOL	E	582	Lübeck find 221.
643	0·91	14·1	↖	—	E	583	Bruun 140.
644	1·24	19·1	↗	—	E	584	Same dies as 645. No provenance.

PLATE 23

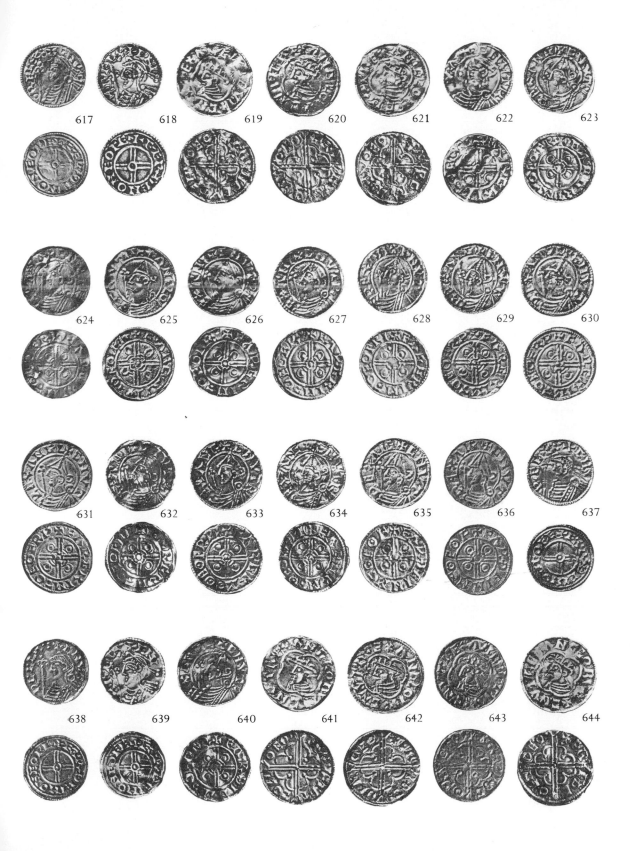

617   618   619   620   621   622   623

624   625   626   627   628   629   630

631   632   633   634   635   636   637

638   639   640   641   642   643   644

PLATE 24

No.	Weight Gm.	Gr.	Die axis	Moneyer	type	Hild. no.	
YORK (contd.)							
645	1·19	18·3	↗	FRIÐCOL	E	584	Same dies as 644. Bruun 141, ex Bille-Brahe.
646	1·10	16·9	↓	—	G	cf. 587 (a 4)	Lübeck find 223.
647	1·05	16·2	↓	—	G	588, rev. 587	Gartz, auction 1901, no. 1168.
648	0·98	15·1	↗	—	G	588, rev. 587	Lübeck find 222.
649	1·09	16·8	←	—	G	589	Same rev. die as 652. Lübeck find 225.
650	1·10	16·9	↓	—	G	590	Beskrivelse 1791, no. 7, R & D 18.
651	1·03	15·9	↗	—	G	590	Enner find 1849.
652	0·93	14·3	↙	—	G	591	Same obv. die as 657; same rev. die as 649. Kirke Værløse find 184.
653	1·01	15·6	↗	—	G	cf. 595	(EOFREI) Store Frigaard find 1928.
654	1·00	15·4	→	—	G	594	Lübeck find 226.
655	1·10	16·9	↗	—	G	595	Lübeck find 227.
656	1·00	15·4	↑	—	G	595	Same obv. die. Bruun 171, ex Bille-Brahe.
657	0·95	14·6	↑	—	G	cf. 597	(EOFERPI) Same obv. die as 652. Lübeck find 228.
658	1·14	17·6	→	—	H	cf. 598	(RECX) Lübeck find 224.
659	1·12	17·3	→	—	H		as 658, but pellet in one angle. Same obv. die. Lübeck find 224.
660	1·01	15·6	↙	GIMVLF	H	599	No provenance.
661	1·09	16·8	↖	—	H	599	No provenance.
662	1·10	16·9	↓	—	H	599	Same dies. Bruun 214, ex Bille-Brahe.
663	1·14	17·6	↖	—	H	599	Bruun 215.
664	1·00	15·4	←	GODMAN	G	o	(AN/EO) Same rev. die as 665–6. Enegaard find 1862.
665	1·04	16·1	→	—	G	o	(ANG/EO) Same dies as 666; same rev. die as 664. Beskrivelse 1791, no. 3. R & D 19.
666	0·97	14·9	↗	—	G	o	(ANG/EO) Same dies as 665; same rev. die as 664. Bruun 172, ex Bille-Brahe.
667	1·13	17·4	↑	—	G	603	Enner find 1849.
668	0·87	13·4	←	—	G	606/604	Lübeck find 230.
669	1·16	17·9	→	—	G	605	Enner find 1849.
670	1·08	16·6	↖	—	G	cf. 607	(Without sceptre.) Bruun 201, ex Ready, auction 1920, no. 140, pl. I.
671	1·08	16·6	←	—	H	613/608	Same dies as 673; same rev. die as 672. Stockholm 1856.
672	1·09	16·8	↖	—	H	614/608	Same rev. die as 671–2. No provenance. Cracked.

PLATE 24

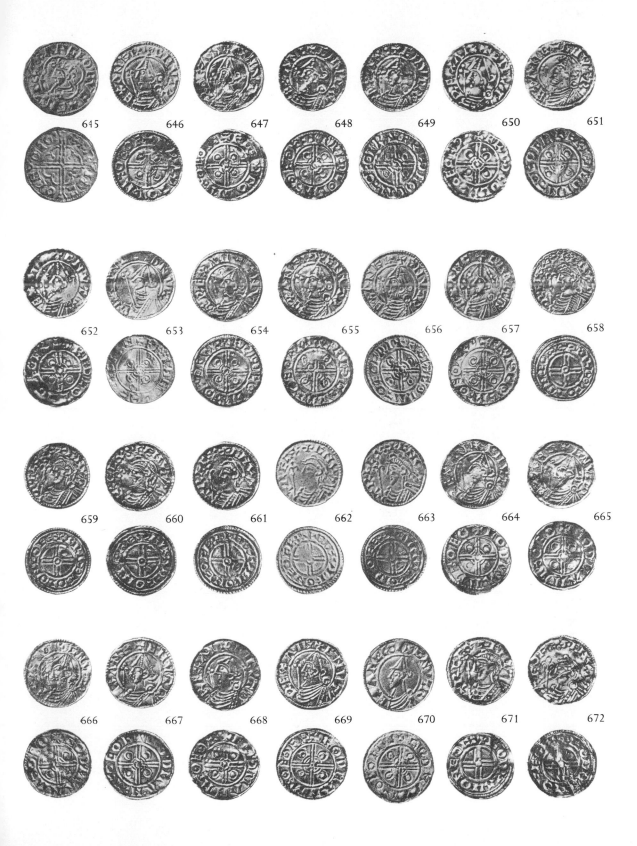

645 646 647 648 649 650 651

652 653 654 655 656 657 658

659 660 661 662 663 664 665

666 667 668 669 670 671 672

PLATE 25

H

No.	Weight		Die axis	Moneyer	type	Hild. no.	
	Gm.	Gr.					

YORK (contd.)

No.	Gm.	Gr.	Die axis	Moneyer	type	Hild. no.	
673	1·03	15·9	↖	GODMAN	H	cf. 608	Same dies as 671; same rev. die as 672. Bruun 216, ex Bille-Brahe.
674	1·10	16·9	→	—	H	612	Same rev. die as 675. Lübeck find 232.
675	1·05	16·2	→	—	H	616/612	Same obv. die as 676 and 679; same rev. die as 674. Lübeck find 233.
676	1·14	17·6	↓	—	H	616/612 var.	Same obv. die as 675 and 679. Bruun 217.
677	1·15	17·7	↑	—	H	614	Store Valby find 1839.
678	1·00	15·4	→	—	H	o	(EOFER) Lübeck find 234.
679	1·13	17·4	→	—	H	616	Same obv. die as 675–6; same rev. die as 680. Siökrona 1883.
680	1·10	16·9	↓	—	H	cf. 616 (b 1)	Same rev. die as 679. Benzon, donation 1885, no. 10.
681	1·08	16·6	↓	—	H	cf. 617 (b)	Hauberg, auction 1929, no. 176.
682	1·09	16·8	↙	—	H	o	(EORC) Bruun 218.
683	1·02	15·7	←	GRIMOLF	G	618	Thomsen 9087.
684	0·90	13·9	→	—	G	618	Same dies. Lübeck find 238.
685	1·01	15·6	↗	—	G	620	Lübeck find 239.
686	0·92	14·2	↗	—	G	cf. 620 (a 1)	Enner find 1849.
687	0·96	14·8	↖	—	G	620/621	Bruun 173, ex Bille-Brahe, ex Stockholm 1854.
688	1·00	15·4	↗	—	G	621/622	Benzon, donation 1885, no. 11.
689	0·99	15·3	↗	—	G	621/622 var.	Lübeck find cf. 238.
690	1·18	18·2	←	GRIMVLF	H	626	Same obv. die as 691–2. Haagerup find 158.
691	1·18	18·2	↓	—	H	627	Same dies as 692; same obv. die as 690. Stolpehuse find 1837.
692	1·07	16·5	↓	—	H	627	Same dies as 691; same obv. die as 690. Bruun 219.
693	0·95	14·6	→	—	H	627/628	Lübeck find 240.
694	0·82	12·6	↙	—	H	630	Stolpehuse find 1837.
695	1·09	16·8	↖	—	I	631	Haagerup find 160.
696	1·03	15·9	↓	GRVCAN	G	cf. 634	(EOF) Lübeck find 242.
697	1·10	16·9	↓	—	H	635	Purchased 1854.
698	1·06	16·3	↑	—	H	cf. 635	(REC) Same rev. die. Lübeck find 243.
699	1·00	15·4	→	GRVRN	G	636	No provenance.
700	1·00	15·4	↖	—	G	636 var.	Same obv. die as 701–2. Store Valby find 1839.

PLATE 25

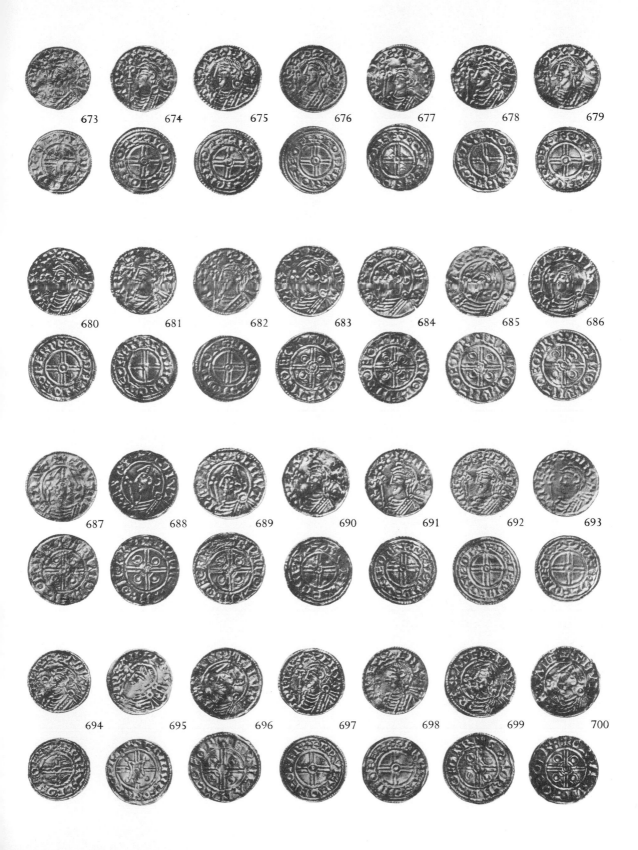

673 674 675 676 677 678 679

680 681 682 683 684 685 686

687 688 689 690 691 692 693

694 695 696 697 698 699 700

PLATE 26

No.	Weight Gm.	Gr.	Die axis	Moneyer	type	Hild. no.	
YORK (contd.)							
701	1·01	15·6	↓	GRVRN	G	637	Same dies as 702; same obv. die as 700; same rev. die as 703. Lübeck find 244.
702	1·03	15·9	↘	—	G	cf. 637	Same dies as 701; same obv. die as 700; same rev. die as 703. Bruun 174.
703	0·97	14·9	→	—	G	cf. 637 (a 2)	Same rev. die as 700–2. Hauberg, auction 1929, no. 159.
704	1·23	19·0	↖	GVNHÞAT	E	638	Lübeck find 245.
705	1·23	19·0	↘	—	E	638 var.	Same obv. die. Lübeck find 246.
706	1·25	19·3	↑	HEARDECNVT	A	639[1]	Bech, auction 1906, no. 71.
707	1·32	20·3	↓	HILDOLF	E	640	Enner find 1849.
708	0·99	15·3	↗	—	E	641	Bruun 142.
709	0·95	14·6	→	—	E	641	Bruun 143. Cracked.
710	0·97	14·9	↙	—	E	642	Ernst, donation 1964, ex Glückstadt, auction 1924, no. 177.
711	0·99	15·3	↗	—	E	643	Store Valby find 1839.
712	1·06	16·3	→	—	E	643	Same rev. die as 714. Enner find 1849.
713	1·22	18·8	↘	—	E	643	Enner find 1849.
714	1·03	15·9	↙	—	E	645	Same rev. die as 712. Beskrivelse 1791, no. 19. R & D 20.
715	1·04	16·1	↑	—	E	645 var.	Bruun 144, ex Bille-Brahe.
716	1·01	15·6	↑	—	E	646	Same obv. die. Enner find 1849.
717	0·96	14·8	←	—	G	cf. 649 (a 2)	Same obv. die as 720. Store Valby find 1839.
718	0·98	15·1	→	—	G	cf. 649	(EOFI) Bonderup find 1854.
719	1·08	16·6	↑	—	G	651	Kongsø plantage find 80.
720	1·00	15·4	↓	—	G	651	Same obv. die as 717. Purchased 1874.
721	0·97	14·9	↖	—	G	653	Thomsen 9090.
722	1·05	16·2	↘	—	G	653	Same dies. Bruun 175.
723	0·97	14·9	↘	—	G	o	(AG) Kongsø plantage find 83.
724	1·10	16·9	↗	—	G	654	Kelstrup find 1859.
725	0·94	14·5	↙	—	G	654	Kongsø plantage find 81.
726	0·99	15·3	←	—	G	654	Ernst donation, 1964.
727	1·14	17·6	↑	—	G	656	Same dies as 728–9. Enner find 1849.
728	1·07	16·5	←	—	G	656	Same dies as 727 and 729. Lübeck find 250.

[1] Scandinavian?—see p. ix.

PLATE 26

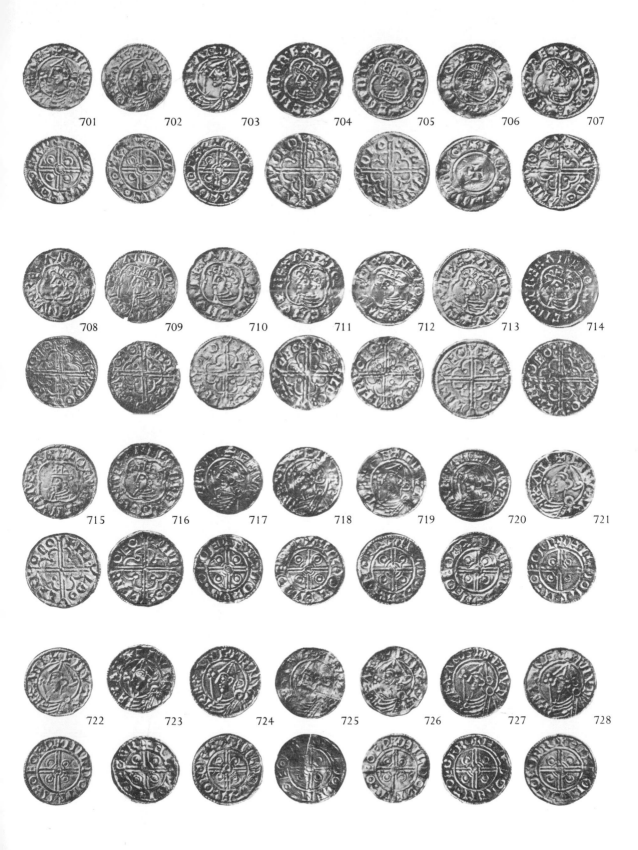

701 702 703 704 705 706 707

708 709 710 711 712 713 714

715 716 717 718 719 720 721

722 723 724 725 726 727 728

PLATE 27

No.	Weight Gm.	Weight Gr.	Die axis	Moneyer	Hild. type	Hild. no.	
YORK (contd.)							
729	0·99	15·3	←	HILDOLF	G	656	Same dies as 727–8. Bruun 176.
730	1·04	16·1	↓	—	G	657	Store Valby find 1839.
731	1·17	18·1	→	—	G	658	Bruun 178.
732	0·97	14·9	↖	—	G	659	Stolpehuse find 1837.
733	0·97	14·9	↙	—	G	659	Same obv. die. Bruun 177. Pierced.
734	1·04	16·1	↘	—	G	660	Bruun 179, ex Bille-Brahe. Cracked.
735	1·01	15·6	↘	—	G	660/661	Store Valby find 1839.
736	1·12	17·3	←	—	G	660/661	Same dies. Bruun 180.
737	1·56	24·1	→	HILDRED	E	666	Stockholm 1861.
738	1·48	22·8	↓	—	E	666	Same dies. Bruun 145.
739	1·07	16·5	↑	HILDVLF	H	668	Same rev. die as 740–1. Thomsen 9091.
740	1·07	16·5	↓	—	H	669	Same dies as 741; same rev. die as 739. Lübeck find 255.
741	1·08	16·6	↘	—	H	669	Same dies as 740; same rev. die as 739. Bruun 220.
742	1·07	16·5	↓	—	H	670	Bruun 221.
743	1·05	16·2	→	—	H	671	Beskrivelse, Tillæg 1794, no. 54, ex Suhm, auction 1802, no. 911. R & D XLVI. Timm, auction 1831, no. 10.
744	1·03	15·9	↖	—	H	674	Gartz, auction 1901, no. 1169.
745	1·13	17·4	↙	—	H	674/676	Same obv. die. Lübeck find 255 a.
746	1·02	15·7	↗	HLDVLF	H	678	Hauberg, auction 1929, no. 177.
747	1·14	17·6	↘	—	H	678	Same rev. die. Bruun 222.
748	0·96	14·8	→	—	H	cf. 678 (a ir. 41)	Same rev. die. Haagerup find 162.
749	1·07	16·5	↘	IIRE	G	0	Same obv. die as 752–3. Lübeck find 256.
750	1·04	16·1	↙	IRE	E	679	Lübeck find 258.
751	0·98	15·1	←	—	G	682	Magnus, donation 1868.
752	1·15	17·7	↗	—	G	683	Same dies as 753; same obv. die as 749. Store Valby find 1839.
753	1·07	16·5	↑	—	G	cf. 683 (a 7)	Same dies as 752; same obv. die as 749. Bruun 181.
754	1·00	15·4	←	—	G	687	Thomsen 9092.
755	1·05	16·2	↓	—	G	688	Lyngby find 1861.
756	1·07	16·5	←	LANDFERÐ	H	0[1]	Beskrivelse 1791, no. 10. R & D 21.

[1] Moneyer not recorded by Hildebrand for the mint for this reign.

PLATE 27

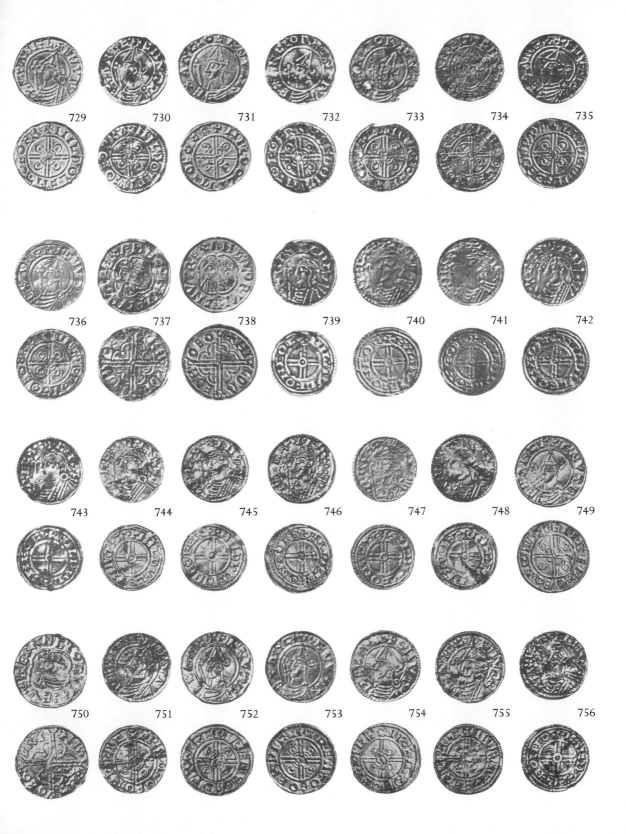

729 730 731 732 733 734 735

736 737 738 739 740 741 742

743 744 745 746 747 748 749

750 751 752 753 754 755 756

PLATE 28

No.	Weight Gm.	Gr.	Die axis	Moneyer	Hild. type	no.	
YORK *(contd.)*							
757	0·99	15·3	↑	LEFƿINE	E	690	Ernst, donation 1964.
758	1·05	16·2	↘	—	E	cf. 690 (a 7)	Lübeck find 261.
759	1·05	16·2	←	—	E	cf. 690 (a 8)	Lübeck find 262.
760	1·03	15·9	↓	—	E	cf. 690 (a 8)	Kelstrup find 1859. Chipped.
761	0·99	15·3	↖	LEFƿIINE	E	cf. 691	Bruun 146, ex Bille-Brahe.
762	1·11	17·1	→	OSCOT	G	cf. 693 (a 5)	Same obv. die as 772. Store Valby find 1839.
763	1·05	16·2	↓	OSGOD	H	694	Lübeck find 264.
764	1·28	19·7	↘	OSGOT	E	696	Ernst, donation 1964, ex Hauberg, auction 1929, no. 144. Cracked.
765	0·96	14·8	→	—	E	698	Stockholm 1861.
766	1·06	16·3	↗	—	E	698	Benzon, donation 1885, no. 12.
767	1·08	16·6	↙	—	E	701	Lyngby find 1861.
768	1·13	17·4	↘	—	E	701	Same rev. die. Bruun 147.
769	0·98	15·1	↗	—	E	701	Kelstrup find 1859.
770	0·89	13·8	↑	—	G	708	Kongsø plantage find 85.
771	1·10	16·9	↓	—	G	cf. 708	(EOFRP) Same dies as 773. Bruun 182.
772	1·04	16·1	↑	—	G	o	Same obv. die as 762. Store Valby find 1839.
773	1·12	17·3	→	—	G	o	Same dies as 771. Enegaard find 1862.
774	0·95	14·6	↙	OSGVTT	E	709	Enner find 1849.
775	0·99	15·3	↑	OSOOT	G	710	Lübeck find 269.
776	1·04	16·1	↑	—	G	710	Same dies. Bruun 183, ex Bille-Brahe, ex O. Thomsen, auction 1880, no. 892.
777	0·90	13·9	↗	OÐAN	H	o	Mann Hartvig, auction 1858, no. 1656, ex Timm, auction 1831, no. 12.
778	1·06	16·3	←	OÐIN	H	713	Same obv. die as 780. Thomsen 9095.
779	1·06	16·3	↘	—	H	713	Same obv. die as 783–4. Haagerup find 163.
780	1·11	17·1	↗	—	H	713	Same obv. die as 778. Bruun 223.
781	1·00	15·4	↓	—	H	713	Haagerup find 164.
782	1·05	16·2	←	—	H	715	Haagerup find 165.
783	1·05	16·2	↗	—	H	716	Same dies as 784 and obv. die as 779. Kongsø plantage find 86.
784	1·11	17·1	↓	—	H	716	Same dies as 783 and same obv. die as 779. Bruun 224.

PLATE 28

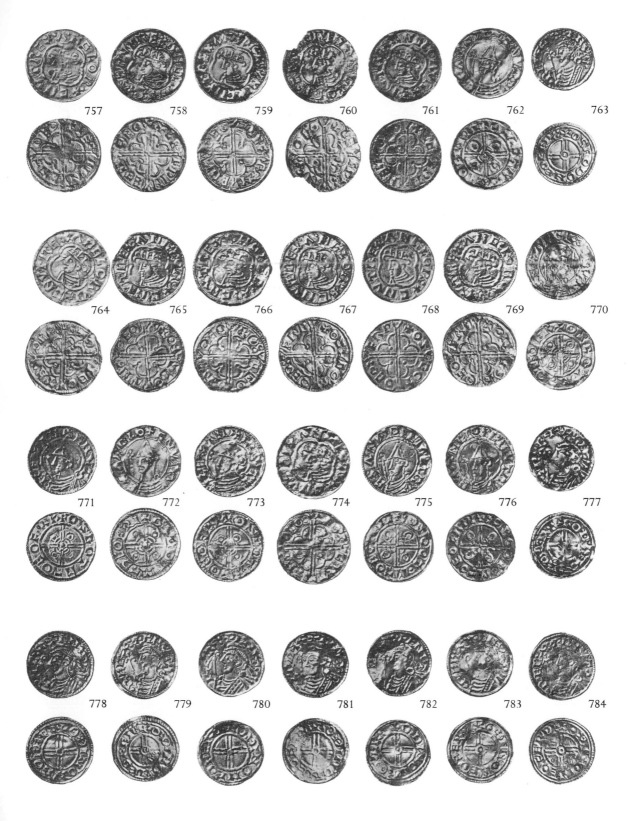

757 758 759 760 761 762 763

764 765 766 767 768 769 770

771 772 773 774 775 776 777

778 779 780 781 782 783 784

PLATE 29

I

No.	Weight Gm.	Gr.	Die axis	Moneyer	type	Hild. no.	
YORK (contd.)							
785	1·14	17·6	←	OÐIN	H	715/716	Gartz, auction 1901, no. 1170.
786	0·96	14·8	→	—	H	0	(EOFIIR) Lübeck find 271.
787	1·05	16·2	←	OÐÐIN	H	718	Lübeck find (not in *ZfN*)
788	1·09	16·8	↓	OVSTMAN	G	719	Bruun 184.
789	1·04	16·1	↓	OVÐGIRM	E	720	No provenance.
790	1·03	15·9	→	OVÐGRIM	E	721	Same rev. die as 789. Bruun 148, ex Bille-Brahe.
791	1·05	16·2	↓	—	E	723	Kelstrup find 1859.
792	1·02	15·7	↓	—	E	724	Bruun 149.
793	1·06	16·3	↙	—	E	cf. 724 (a, ir. 113)	Lübeck find 274.
794	1·06	16·3	→	RÆFEN	H	726	Same obv. die as 795–6, 798; same rev. die as 797. Munksjørup find 1829.
795	1·03	15·9	↓	—	H	726	Same dies as 796; same obv. die as 794 and 798. Haagerup find 166.
796	1·09	16·8	↑	—	H	726	Same dies as 795; same obv. die as 794 and 798. Bruun 225.
797	1·05	16·2	↖	—	H	728	Same rev. die as 794. Haagerup find 167.
798	1·08	16·6	↙	—	H	731	Same obv. die as 794–6. Lübeck find 277.
799	0·98	15·1	↑	—	H	733	Haagerup find 168.
800	1·14	17·6	↓	—	H	734	Same dies as 801; same obv. die as 802. Lübeck find 278.
801	1·09	16·8	↖	—	H	734	Same dies as 800; same obv. die as 802. Bruun 226, ex Bille-Brahe, ex Stockholm 1854.
802	1·10	16·9	↑	—	H	cf. 735 (b)	Same obv. die as 800–1. Thomsen 9096.
803	1·01	15·6	←	SCVLAA	I	738	Beskrivelse, Tillæg 1794, no. 42, ex Suhm, auction 1802, no. 899. R & D 24.
804	0·99	15·3	←	—	I	738	Same dies. Bruun 235.
805	1·08	16·6	↓	SELECOL	E	740	Enner find 1849.
806	1·05	16·2	↑	—	E	cf. 740 (a 7)	Kelstrup find 1859.
807	1·07	16·5	↑	—	E	cf. 740 (a 8)	Bruun 150, ex Bille-Brahe.
808	1·05	16·2	↙	—	E	cf. 740	(EOFRPIC) Lübeck find 282.
809	0·99	15·3	↙	—	E	741	Lübeck find 281.
810	1·04	16·1	↙	SNECOL	E	744	Lübeck find 283.
811	1·27	19·6	↓	STIRCAR	E	0 (cf. 750)	Kelstrup find 1859.
812	1·07	16·5	↖	STIRCER	E	749	Same obv. die as 813. Siökrona 1883.

PLATE 29

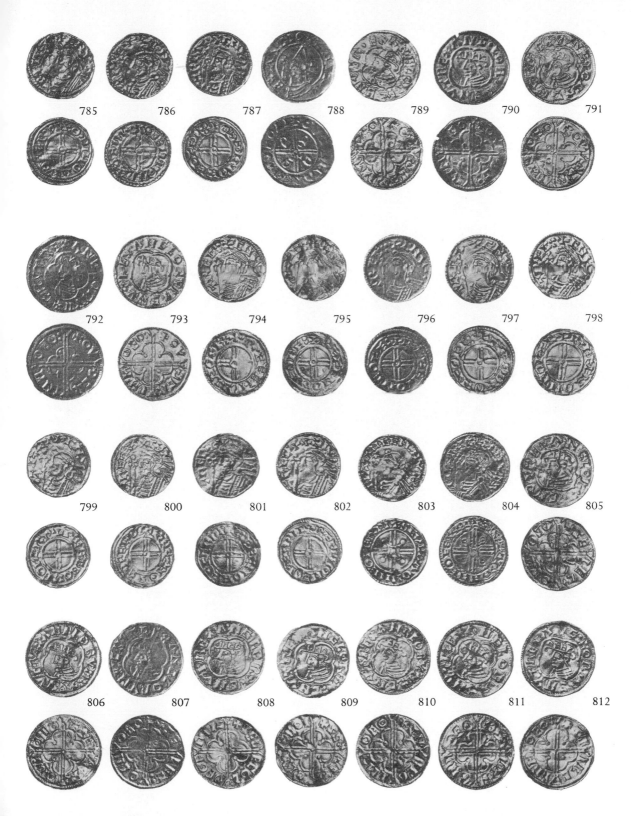

785   786   787   788   789   790   791

792   793   794   795   796   797   798

799   800   801   802   803   804   805

806   807   808   809   810   811   812

PLATE 30

No.	Weight Gm.	Gr.	Die axis	Moneyer	type	Hild. no.	
YORK (*contd.*)							
813	1·00	15·4	↗	STIRCER	E	751	Same obv. die as 812. Stockholm 1854.
814	1·12	17·3	↙	STIRCOL	E	753	Kelstrup find 1859.
815	0·96	14·8	→	—	E	753	Same dies. Bruun 151, ex Bille-Brahe, ex Thomsen 9097.
816	1·05	16·2	↗	—	E	753	Enner find 1849.
817	1·29	19·9	↖	—	E	753	Bruun 152.
818	1·00	15·4	↑	—	E	758	Enner find 1849.
819	1·16	17·9	↙	—	G	759	Same obv. die as 820, 822, and 826. Enner find 1849.
820	1·16	17·9	→	—	G	760	Same obv. die as 819, 822, and 826; same rev. die as 823. Lübeck find 285.
821	1·03	15·9	→	—	G	760	Bruun 185.
822	0·99	15·3	↙	—	G	760	Same obv. die as 819–20 and 826. Store Valby find 1839.
823	1·09	16·8	↗	—	G	761	Same rev. die as 820. Thomsen 9098.
824	1·05	16·2	↘	—	G	cf. 762 (a, ir. 96)	Enner find 1849.
825	1·15	17·7	→	—	G	cf. 762	Same dies. Bruun 186.
826	1·10	16·9	↘	—	G	763	Same obv. die as 819–20 and 822. Beskrivelse, Tillæg 1794, p. 11, no. 45, ex Suhm, auction 1802, no. 902. R & D 22.
827	(0·96)	(14·8)	↖	STIRCOLL	I	764	Haagerup find 169. Damaged.
828	1·14	17·6	↘	—	I	764	Same dies. Bruun 236.
829	0·96	13·2	→	STRCOL	G	cf. 765 (a 4)	Bruun 187.
830	1·03	15·9	↑	SVINOLF	E	767	Same obv. die as 831–3. Bruun 153.
831	1·03	15·9	↘	SVNOLF	E	769	Same obv. die as 830 and 832–3. Stockholm 1854.
832	1·02	15·7	↗	—	E	769	Same obv. die as 830–1 and 833. Lübeck find (cf. 292).
833	(0·81)	(12·5)	←	—	E	cf. 760	(MIOEO) Same obv. die as 830–3. Beskrivelse, Tillæg 1794, p. 10, no. 31. R & D 23. Damaged.
834	1·04	16·1	↘	—	E	772	Bruun 154.
835	1·38	21·3	→	—	E	776	Lübeck find 291.
836	1·26	19·4	↓	—	E	776	Same dies. Bruun 155.
837	0·97	14·9	→	—	G	cf. 777 (a 2)	Enner find 1849.
838	1·03	15·9	→	—	G	cf. 777 (a 2)	Bruun 188, ex Bille-Brahe.
839	0·99	15·3	↖	—	G	778	Lübeck find 288.
840	0·98	15·1	↗	—	G	778	Bruun 189.

PLATE 30

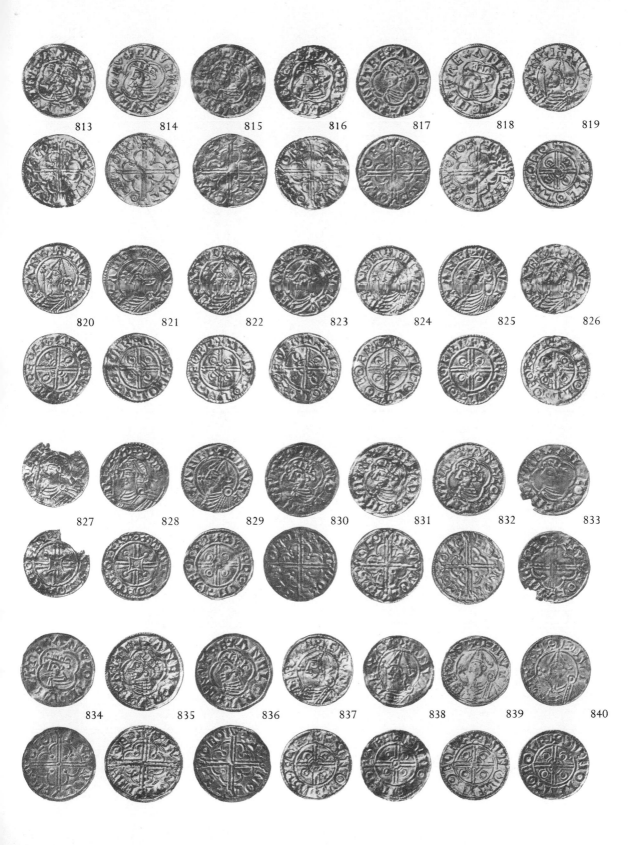

813   814   815   816   817   818   819

820   821   822   823   824   825   826

827   828   829   830   831   832   833

834   835   836   837   838   839   840

PLATE 31

No.	Weight Gm.	Gr.	Die axis	Moneyer	type	Hild. no.	
841	0·99	15·3	↙	SVNOLF	G	779	Haagerup find 170.
842	1·00	15·4	↗	—	G	cf. 779 (a ir. 81)	Lübeck find 289.
843	1·14	17·6	←	—	G	784	Kelstrup find 1859.
844	0·95	14·6	↖	—	G	785	Thomsen 9100.
845	1·04	16·1	↑	SVNVLF	E	789	Bonderup find 1854.
846	1·08	16·6	↙	—	E	789	Same dies. Bruun 156, ex Bille-Brahe.
847	1·11	17·1	↙	—	H	791	Lübeck find 294.
848	0·99	15·3	↓	SVRTINC	G	792	Store Valby find 1839.
849	0·92	14·2	→	—	G	cf. 792 (obv. retrograde, legend blundered)	Bruun 190.
850	0·95	14·6	↑	—	G	793	Same dies as 850; same obv. die as 852. Store Valby find 1839.
851	0·95	14·6	↑	—	G	793	Same dies as 850; same obv. die as 852. Bruun 191, ex Bille-Brahe.
852	1·01	15·6	↓	—	G	cf. 793	(EO) Kongsø plantage find 89.
853	1·12	17·3	↑	SPEGEN	I	795	Bruun 237.
854	1·02	15·7	↓	SPERTINC	E	796	Same obv. die as 859. Kelstrup find 1859.
855	1·16	17·9	↘	—	E	797	Hauberg, auction 1929, no. 148.
856	1·35	20·8	↙	—	E	797	Same obv. die. Bruun 157.
857	1·26	19·4	←	—	E	798	Stockholm 1846.
1504	1·27	19·6	↙	—	E	798	Same dies. Bruun 158, ex Bille-Brahe, ex Thomsen 9102. (Plate 54.)
858	1·07	16·5	↖	—	E	800	Kelstrup find 1859.
859	1·04	16·1	↙	—	E	cf. 801	(IO) Same obv. die as 854. Lübeck find 295.
860	0·93	14·3	↖	SPERTNC	G	cf. 802	Enner find 1849.
861	0·97	14·9	↘	ÐVRGRIM	H	803	Lübeck find 296.
862	0·94	14·5	↙	—	H	803	Bruun 227, ex Bille-Brahe.
863	1·09	16·8	←	—	H	804	Bonderup find 1854.
864	0·86	13·2	↘	—	H	805	Hauberg, auction 1929, no. 182.
865	1·06	16·3	↖	—	H	805	Same rev. die as 867. Bruun 228.
866	1·02	15·7	↗	—	H	805	Schou, auction 1926, no. 21.
867	1·09	16·8	↓	—	H	805	Same rev. die as 865. No provenance.
868	1·06	16·3	↓	—	H	807	Same rev. die as 869. Lübeck find 297.

PLATE 31

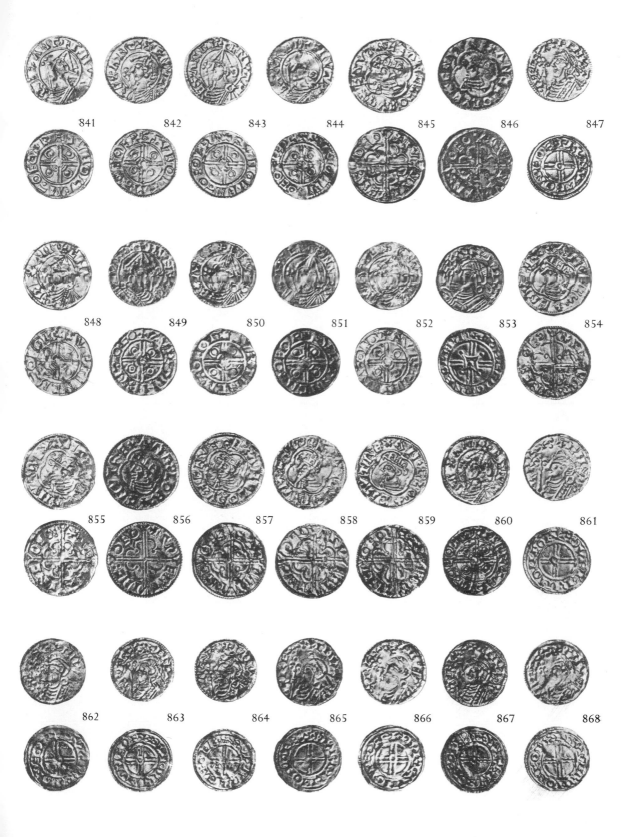

841 842 843 844 845 846 847

848 849 850 851 852 853 854

855 856 857 858 859 860 861

862 863 864 865 866 867 868

PLATE 32

No.	Weight Gm.	Gr.	Die axis	Moneyer	Hild. type	Hild. no.	
YORK (contd.)							
869	1·03	15·9	↓	ÐVRGRIM	H	808	Same rev. die as 868. Nielsen 1853.
870	1·08	16·6	↑	TOCA	G	812	Bech, auction 1906, no. 91.
871	1·05	16·2	↘	—	G	812	Same dies. Bruun 192.
872	1·01	15·6	↑	TOCAA	E	cf. 813 (a 5)	Lübeck find 300.
873	1·06	16·3	↖	TOOCA	G	814	Same obv. die as 876–7. Enner find 1849.
874	0·97	14·9	↘	—	G	815	Same dies as 875; same obv. die as 879. Enner find 1849.
875	1·07	16·5	↙	—	G	815	Same dies as 874; same obv. die as 879. Bruun 193.
876	1·10	16·9	↖	—	G	816	Same obv. die as 873 and 877. Kelstrup find 1859.
877	1·05	16·2	↓	—	G	816	Same obv. die as 873 and 876. Stolpehuse find 1837.
878	1·10	16·9	↗	—	G	cf. 816 (a 4)	Lübeck find 303.
879	1·05	16·2	←	—	G	cf. 816	Same obv. die as 874–5. Bruun 194, ex Bille-Brahe.
880	0·95	14·6	↘	VCEDE	H	817	Lübeck find 304.
881	1·09	16·8	↗	—	H	818	Same obv. die as 886–7. Beskrivelse, Tillæg 1794, p. 9, no. 14. R & D 26.
882	1·13	17·4	↘	—	H	818	Same obv. die as 883–4, Bruun 229.
883	1·08	16·6	↓	—	H	821	Same dies as 884; same obv. die as 882. R & D 26 a.
884	1·12	17·3	↓	—	H	821	Same dies as last. Enner find 1849.
885	1·10	16·9	↙	—	H	824	Beskrivelse, Tillæg 1794, p. 9, no. 15. R & D 27.
886	0·98	15·1	↙	—	H	824	Same die as 887; same obv. die as 881; same rev. die as 888. Bruun 230, ex Bille-Brahe, ex Stockholm 1854.
887	1·10	16·9	→	—	H	824	Same as last. Ernst, donation 1964.
888	1·17	18·1	←	—	H	825	Store Valby find 1839.
889	1·13	17·4	↙	VCEDEE	I	826	Haagerup find 171.
890	1·30	20·1	↙	VLFCETEL	E	827	Haagerup find 172.
891	1·11	17·1	↗	—	E	cf. 827 (a 8)	Hess, auction 1891, no. 929.
892	1·07	16·5	↘	VLFGRIM	E	830	Enner find 1849.
893	1·07	16·5	←	—	E	834	Same obv. die as 894–5. Enner find 1849. Pierced.
894	1·07	16·5	→	—	E	834	Same obv. die as 893 and 895. Bruun 159, ex Bille-Brahe.
895	1·00	15·4	↓	—	E	834/833	Same obv. die as 893–4. R & D Tillæg T. I. 27 a.
896	1·03	15·9	↗	—	E	o (a 5, 10)	Lübeck find 310.

PLATE 32

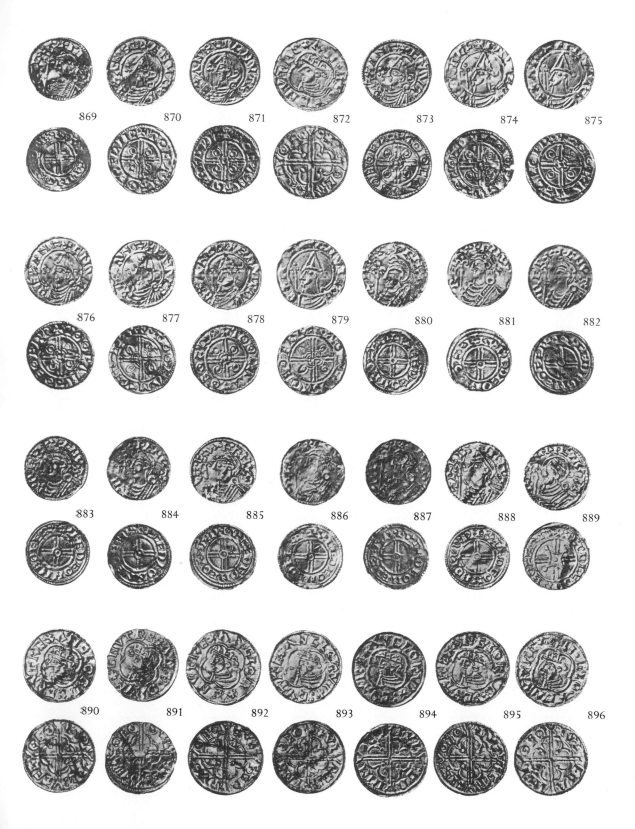

869 870 871 872 873 874 875

876 877 878 879 880 881 882

883 884 885 886 887 888 889

890 891 892 893 894 895 896

PLATE 33

No.	Weight Gm.	Weight Gr.	Die axis	Moneyer	Hild. type	Hild. no.	
YORK (contd.)							
897	0·97	14·4	↙	VLFGARIM	E	836	Lübeck find 309.
898	0·99	15·3	↙	VLFNOÐ	G	o	Lübeck find 308.
899	0·87	13·4	↑	ÞIÐRIN	G	840	Kongsø plantage find 90.
900	0·93	14·3	↙	—	G	840	Same dies. Bruun 195.
901	1·03	15·9	↖	—	G	842	Thomsen 9108.
902	1·01	15·6	↖	ÞIÐRINE	G	843	Lübeck find 312.
903	1·03	15·9	↖	—	G	843	Stockholm 1854.
904	1·11	17·1	↗	ÞVLFNOÐ	G	cf. 846 (a 3)	Kelstrup find 1859.
905	0·96	14·8	→	—	G	o	(EOFI) Lübeck find 313.
906	1·07	16·5	↑	—	G	cf. 856 (a 5)	Kelstrup find 1859.
907	1·02	15·7	←	ÞVLNOÐ	G	cf. 850	(EOF:) Same obv. die as 908. R & D LV, ex Frost, auction 1827, no. 16 (sic!).
908	0·97	14·9]	→	—	G	850	Same obv. die. Kongsø plantage find 92.
909	0·95	14·6	↖	—	G	850	Same obv. die as 910. Bruun 196, ex Bille-Brahe.
910	0·96	14·8	→	—	G	850	Same obv. die. Bruun 197.
911	1·12	17·3	↗	—	G	854	Lübeck find 317.
912	0·98	15·1	↙	—	G	cf. 855 (a ir. 87)	Bruun 198.
913	0·97	14·9	→	—	G	857	Store Valby find 1839.
914	1·12	17·3	↖	—	H	861	Same dies as 915; same rev. die as 916. Kongsø plantage find 93.
915	1·08	16·6	←	—	H	861	Same dies as 914; same rev. die as 916. Bruun 231, ex Bille-Brahe.
916	1·13]	17·4	↙	—	H	863	Same obv. die as 917; Same rev. die as 914–15. Lübeck find 315.
917	1·09	16·8	↖	—	H	863/864	Lübeck find 315 (sic!).
918	(0·67)	(10·3)	↑	(ÞVLSI)GE	Aa	(E/A) 865[1]	Store Frigaard find 1928. Cut halfpenny.
919	1·06	16·3	←	ÞVLSTAN	E	cf. 866 (a ir. 113/MO)	Enner find 1849.
920	0·99	15·3	↗	—	E	cf. 867 (a ir. 113)	Same obv. die. Bruun 160, ex Bille-Brahe.
921	1·10	16·9	↗	—	E	cf. 867 (a 7/EOF)	Lübeck find 320.
922	1·05	16·2	↗	—	G	cf. 868 (a 4)	Same dies as 925. Store Valby find 1839.
923	0·99	15·3	↘	—	G	cf. 869 (a ir. 74)	Bruun 199.
924	1·06	16·3	↑	—	G	870	Kelstrup find 1859.

[1] Scandinavian?—see p. ix.

PLATE 33

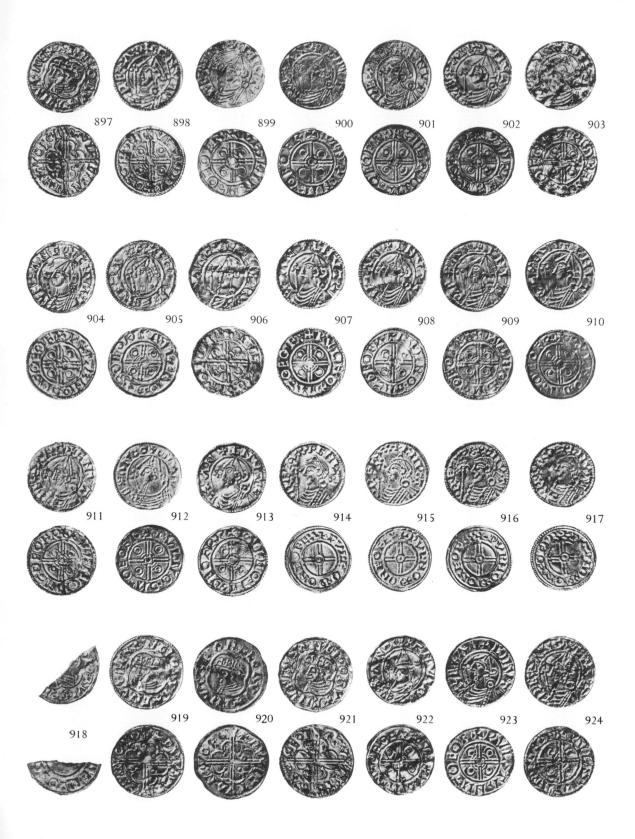

897 898 899 900 901 902 903

904 905 906 907 908 909 910

911 912 913 914 915 916 917

918 919 920 921 922 923 924

PLATE 34

No.	Weight Gm.	Weight Gr.	Die axis	Moneyer	Hild. type	Hild. no.	
YORK (contd.)							
925	1·05	16·2	→	ꝥVLSTAN	G	cf. 871	Same dies as 922. Bruun 200.
926	1·16	17·9	↓	—	G	872	Lübeck find 321.
927	1·03	15·9	↑	—	G	873	Same obv. die. Haagerup find 173.
928	1·01	15·6	↓	—	G	cf. 873 (a 2)	Enner find 1849.
GIFELCEASTER (ILCHESTER)							
929	1·02	15·7	↓	ÆGELꝥIG	G	o[1]	(GIFE) Enner find 1849.
930	1·08	16·6	↓	—	G	o[1]	Same dies. Bruun 244.
931	0·97	14·9	↑	—	G	o[1]	(GIFEL) Siökrona 1883.
932	1·06	16·3	←	—	H	cf. 874 (a)	Haagerup find 174.
933	1·09	16·8	→	ÆLFNOÐ	G	o[2]	Bruun 245, ex Bille-Brahe.
934	1·06	16·3	→	—	G	o[2]	Same dies. Store Valby find 1839.
935	0·94	14·5	↓	ÆLFSIG	E	877	Same obv. die as 940. Kelstrup find 1859.
936	0·89	13·7	←	—	E	cf. 877 (a 7)	Benzon, donation 1885, no. 13.
937	0·82	12·6	→	ÆLFSIGE	E	878	Kelstrup find 1859.
938	0·90	13·9	↑	—	E	879	Kelstrup find 1859.
939	0·88	13·6	←	—	E	881	Stockholm 1885.
940	1·08	16·6	↓	ÆLFSIIG	E	o	Same obv. die as 935. Lübeck find 328.
941	0·78	12·1	→	ÆLFꝥINE	E	cf. 883 (a 8/ON)	Store Frigaard find 1928.
942	0·95	14·6	↓	—	E	884	Same obv. die. Siökrona 1883.
943	0·88	13·6	→	—	E	cf. 884	(ON) Benzon, donation 1885, no. 14.
944	1·03	15·9	→	—	E	885	Kelstrup find 1859.
945	0·86	13·2	↗	—	E	885	Bruun 238.
946	1·14	17·6	↑	—	E	o	Store Valby find 1839.
947	1·11	17·1	←	—	G	o	Same obv. die as 949–50. Enner find 1849.
948	1·10	16·9	→	—	G	o	Lübeck find 329.
949	1·16	17·9	←	ÆLFꝥINE MVS͵	G	891	Same dies as 950; same obv. die as 947. Lübeck find 330.
950	1·09	16·8	↓	—	G	o	Same dies as 949; same obv. die as 947. Bruun 246, ex Bille-Brahe.
951	1·25	19·3	→	ÆÐELMÆR	E	o	Thomsen 9112.
952	1·13	17·4	→	CÆFEL	H	895	Bruun 247.

[1] Moneyer not recorded by Hildebrand for the type.
[2] Moneyer not recorded by Hildebrand for the mint in this reign.

PLATE 34

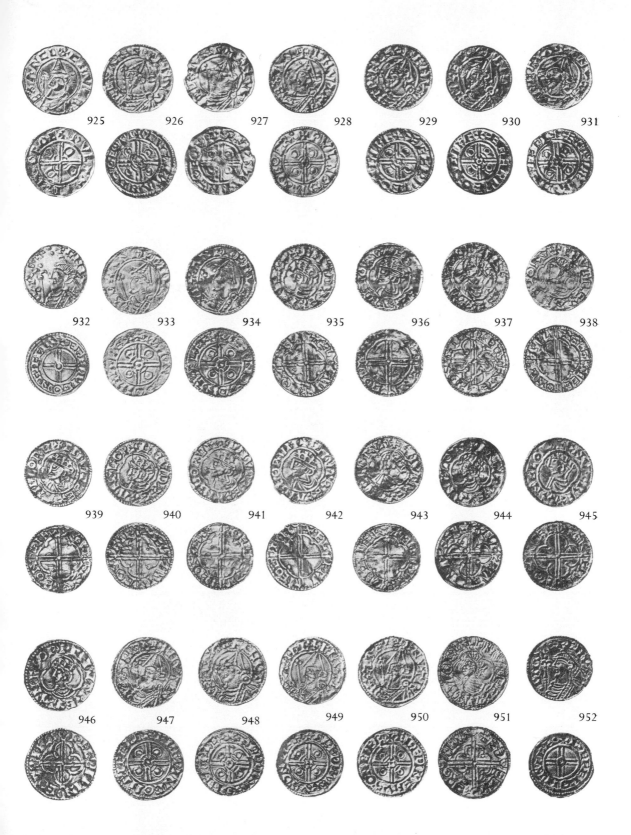

925 926 927 928 929 930 931

932 933 934 935 936 937 938

939 940 941 942 943 944 945

946 947 948 949 950 951 952

PLATE 35

No.	Weight Gm.	Weight Gr.	Die axis	Moneyer	Hild. type	Hild. no.	
ILCHESTER (cont.)							
953	0·91	14·1	↓	GODPINE	E	900	Lübeck find 331.
954	0·90	13·9	→	—	E	900	Same obv. die. Bruun 239, ex Bille-Brahe, ex Siökrona 1883.
955	0·82	12·6	→	OSPI	E	903	Enner find 1849.
956	0·94	14·5	↑	—	E	904	Enner find 1849.
957	0·78	12·1	←	—	E	cf. 906	(GIFEL) Same obv. die as 960. Bruun 240, ex Bille-Brahe.
958	0·89	13·7	→	—	E	906	Haagerup find 175.
959	1·03	15·9	↘	—	E	906	Bruun 241.
960	0·79	12·2	→	—	E	cf. 911	(GIFLC) Same obv. die as 957. Thomsen 9113.
961	1·06	16·3	→	—	E	911	Stockholm 1885.
962	1·06	16·3	→	—	E	cf. 911 (a 8)	Enner find 1849.
963	0·85	13·1	↑	OSPIE	E	913	Enner find 1849.
964	0·90	13·9	↓	—	E	cf. 914 (a 6)	Purchased 1854.
965	0·90	13·9	↓	—	E	914	Lübeck find 332.
966	0·88	13·6	↖	—	E	914	Same dies. Bruun 242.
967	1·12	17·3	↑	PVLFELM	E	916	Lübeck find 333.
968	1·05	16·2	↑	—	E	918.	No provenance.
969	1·07	16·5	↗	—	E	918	Same dies. Bruun 243.
970	0·99	15·3	↑	—	E	923	Stockholm 1885.
GIPESPIC (IPSWICH)							
971	1·03	15·9	↓	ÆGELBRIH	G	o[1]	Lübeck find 334.
972	1·08	16·6	↓	—	G	o[1]	Same dies. Kelstrup find 1859.
973	1·18	18·2	↓	ÆGLBIRIHT	H	924	Lübeck find 326.
974	1·14	17·6	↓	—	H	924	Same dies. Bruun 257, ex Bille-Brahe.
975	1·09	16·8	↓	ÆÐELBERHT	E	927	Lübeck find 335.
976	1·08	16·6	↑	ÆÐELBRHT	E	930	Kelstrup find 1859.
977	0·90	13·9	↘	BRANTINC	E	o (a 4)[2]	Benzon, donation 1885, no. 15.
978	0·88	13·6	↖	—	E	o (a 6)[2]	Same rev. die as 979–80. Store Valby find 1839.
979	0·90	13·9	↓	—	E	o[2]	Same dies as 980; same rev. die as 978. Enner find 1849.
980	0·91	14·1	↙	—	E	o[2]	Same dies as 979; same rev. die as 978. Bruun 248, ex Bille-Brahe, ex Siökrona 1883.

[1] Moneyer not recorded by Hildebrand for the type.
[2] Moneyer not recorded by Hildebrand for the mint in this reign, but the name occurs at Sudbury in this type.

PLATE 35

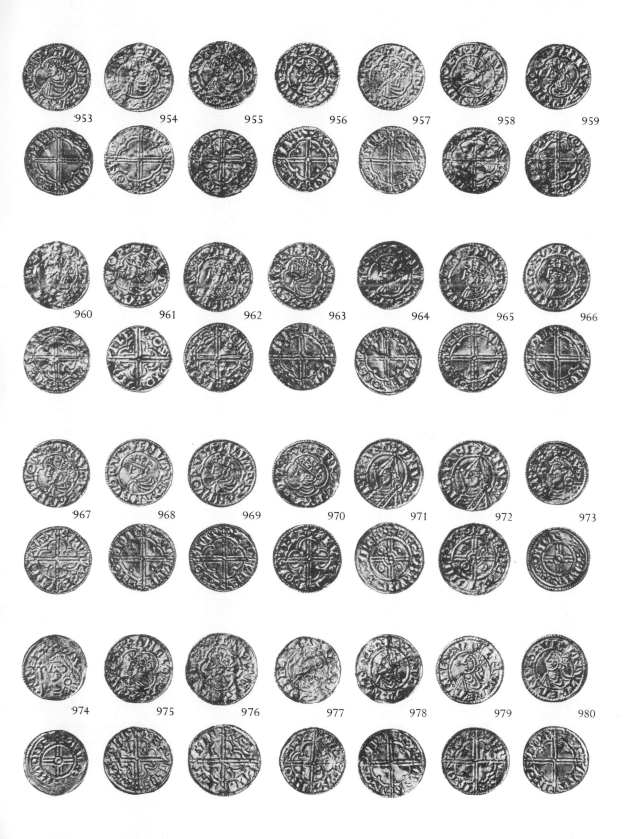

953 954 955 956 957 958 959

960 961 962 963 964 965 966

967 968 969 970 971 972 973

974 975 976 977 978 979 980

PLATE 36

No.	Weight Gm.	Weight Gr.	Die axis	Moneyer	type	Hild. no.	
IPSWICH (*contd.*)							
981	0·86	13·2	↖	BRANTINC	E	o[1]	Variant with cross before face. Bruun 249.
982	1·02	15·7	↖	EDEIIC	E	o	Bruun 251.
983	1·09	16·8	→	EDRIC	E	933	Thomsen 9115.
984	1·03	15·9	↓	—	E	cf. 935 (a 10)	Enner find 1849.
985	1·07	16·5	↓	—	E	cf. 935	Same dies. Stockholm 1885.
986	1·04	16·1	↖	—	E	cf. 935	Same dies. Bruun 250.
987	0·88	13·6	↓	—	E	cf. 937 (a ir. 102)	Hess 1891.
988	1·05	16·2	↑	—	G	938	Store Valby find 1839.
989	1·07	16·5	→	—	G	938	Same dies. Kelstrup find 1859.
990	1·05	16·2	←	—	G	939	Same dies as 991; same obv. die as 992. Enner find 1849.
991	1·04	16·1	→	—	G	939	Same dies as 990; same obv. die as 992. Bruun 254, ex Bille-Brahe.
992	1·11	17·1	→	—	G	cf. 939	(ONNGIPES:) Same obv. die as 990–1. Lübeck find 336.
993	0·99	15·3	↓	GCRLAF	G	cf. 942 (a 3)	Same obv. die as 994–5. Kelstrup find 1859.
994	1·04	16·1	→	GOTSALIN	G	943	Same dies as 995; same obv. die as 993. Enner find 1849.
995	1·07	16·5	→	—	G	943	Same dies as 994; same obv. die as 993. Bruun 255.
996	1·21	18·6	↘	LEMON	E	o[2]	Bruun 253.
997	1·15	17·7	↙	LEOFRIC	E	945	Bruun 252.
998	1·14	17·6	→	—	I	o[3]	Bruun 259.
999	1·28	19·7	←	LEOFꝥINE	E	o[2]	Kelstrup find 1859.
1000	1·19	18·3	↓	—	G	o[2]	Enner find 1849.
1001	1·39	21·4	←	LIFIC	E	o	Bonderup find 1854.
1002	1·29	19·9	←	—	E	o	Same dies. Bech, auction 1906, no. 108.
1003	1·11	17·1	↑	LIFINC	G	949	Same obv. die as 1006. Curt, London 1858.
1004	1·20	18·5	→	—	H	951	Purchased 1854.
1005	1·15	17·7	→	—	H	951	Same dies. Bruun 258.
1006	1·04	16·1	↓	LIFINCC	G	952	Same obv. die as 1003. Store Frigaard find 1928.
1007	1·09	16·8	←	LIIFINC	G	953	Store Valby find 1839.
1008	1·09	16·8	→	—	G	953	Same dies. Bruun 256.

[1] See note on preceding page.
[2] Moneyer not recorded by Hildebrand for mint in this reign.
[3] Moneyer not recorded by Hildebrand for the type.

PLATE 36

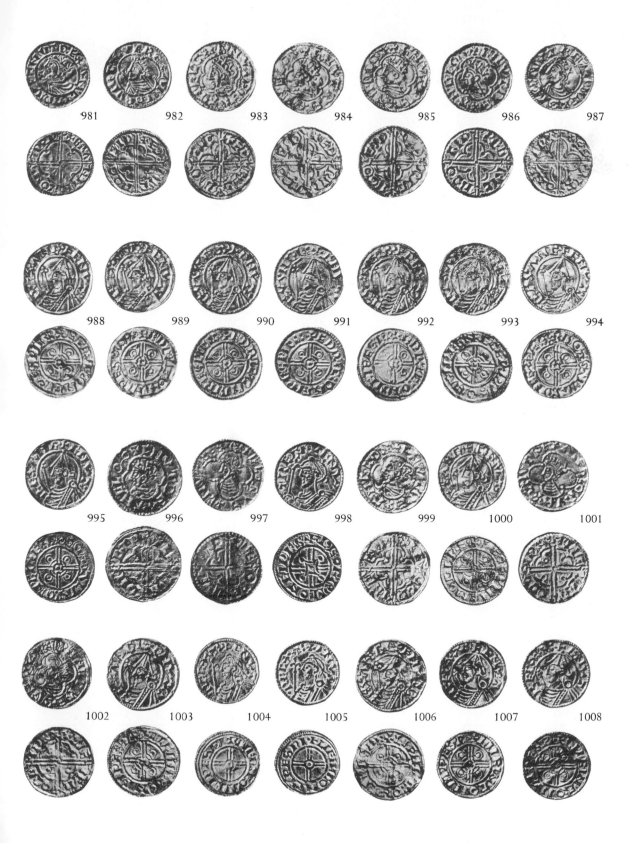

981 982 983 984 985 986 987

988 989 990 991 992 993 994

995 996 997 998 999 1000 1001

1002 1003 1004 1005 1006 1007 1008

PLATE 37

L

No.	Weight Gm.	Weight Gr.	Die axis	Moneyer	Hild. type	Hild. no.	
IPSWICH (*contd.*)							
1009	1·04	16·1	↓	LYFINC	E	956	Kelstrup find 1859.
1010	1·28	19·7	→	ODEA	E	957	Store Valby find 1839.
GLEAÞECEASTER (GLOUCESTER)							
1011	1·15	17·7	→	ÆGELRIC	H	958	Kongsø plantage find 94.
1012	1·12	17·3	→	ÆLRIC	H	o	Haagerup find 178.
1013	0·94	14·5	↑	BOLLA	E	961	Curt, London 1858.
1014	1·12	17·3	→	—	G	963	Kelstrup find 1859.
1015	1·11	17·1	→	—	G	963	Same dies. Bruun 266.
1016	1·12	17·3	↑	—	G	964	Kelstrup find 1859.
1017	1·02	15·7	↑	—	G	cf. 964	Same obv. die. (GLEPEC—Pellet at each end of the cross.) Thomsen 9117.
1018	1·00	15·4	↓	GODRIC	Ed	cf. 966 (a 4)	Same rev. die as 1019–20. Store Valby find 1839.
1019	1·16	17·9	→	—	Ed	966	Same dies as 1020; same rev. die as 1018. Store Valby find 1839.
1020	1·18	18·2	↙	—	Ed	966	Same dies as 1019; same rev. die as 1018. Bruun 264.
1021	1·03	15·9	→	—	G	967	Lübeck find 341.
1022	1·04	16·1	←	—	G	967	Same dies. Bruun 267.
1023	1·13	17·4	↑	—	G	968	Enner find 1849.
1024	1·12	17·3	←	—	G	968	Same dies. Bruun 268.
1025	1·17	18·1	↓	—	H	970	Thomsen 9119. R & D Tillæg T. I. Lix*a*.
1026	1·15	17·7	←	GODRICC	G	972	Siökrona 1883.
1027	1·12	17·3	↑	GODÞINE	E	973	Lübeck find 344.
1028	1·10	16·9	↑	—	E	973	Same dies. Bruun 261. Slightly chipped.
1029	1·22	18·8	↓	—	E	o	Same dies as 1030; same obv. die as 1031. ∴ before face. Beskrivelse, Tillæg 1794, p. 10, no. 19. R & D 29.
1030	1·28	19·7	↙	—	E	o	Same dies as 1029; same obv. die as 1031. Bruun 260.
1031	1·15	17·7	↙	—	E	o	Same obv. die as 1029–30. Enner find 1849.
1032	1·11	17·1	↓	—	Ec	cf. 976/974	(Var. with sceptre.) Bruun 263.
1033	1·05	16·2	↑	—	G	979	Haagerup find 180. Cracked.
1034	1·07	16·5	↓	LEOFNOÐ	G	980	Bech, auction 1906, no. 114.
1035	1·20	18·5	←	—	H	cf. 981	(GLE) Bruun 269.
1036	1·14	17·6	↗	LEOFSIGE	E	983	Same dies as 1037; same obv. die as 1038. Cross before face. Beskrivelse, Tillæg 1794, no. 28. R & D 30.

PLATE 37

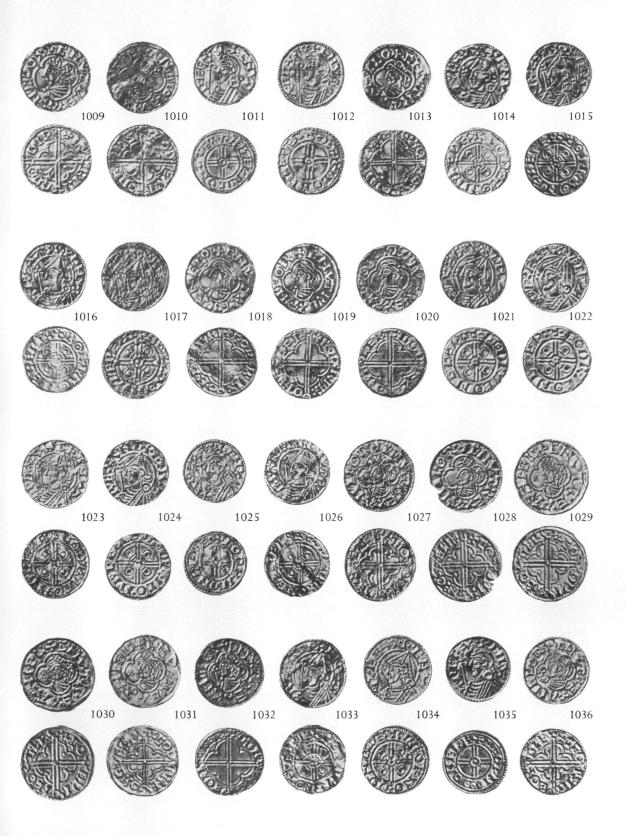

1009   1010   1011   1012   1013   1014   1015

1016   1017   1018   1019   1020   1021   1022

1023   1024   1025   1026   1027   1028   1029

1030   1031   1032   1033   1034   1035   1036

PLATE 38

No.	Weight Gm.	Gr.	Die axis	Moneyer	Hild. type	no.	

GLOUCESTER (contd.)

No.	Gm.	Gr.	Die axis	Moneyer	type	no.	
1037	1·09	16·8	↑	LEOFSIGE	E	983	Same dies as 1036; same obv. die as 1038. Bruun 262.
1038	(0·78)	(12·1)	↖	—	E	983	Same obv. die as 1036–7. Hauberg, auction 1929, no. 190.
1039	1·11	17·1	↑	—	E	985	Enner find 1849.
1040	1·09	16·6	↖	—	Ed	o	(Diademed head.) Bruun 265.
1041	1·10	16·9	→	—	G	o[1]	Kelstrup find 1859.
1042	1·14	17·6	↓	—	G	o[1]	Haagerup find 181.
1043	1·13	17·4	↓	SIRED	E	cf. 987	Pellet before face. Kelstrup find 1859.
1044	1·07	16·5	↓	—	E	988	ω before face, rev. cross in one quarter. Siökrona 1883.
1045	1·07	16·5	↓	—	E	cf. 988	Same obv. die. (Rev. without cross.) Kelstrup find 1859.
1046	1·11	17·1	→	—	E	o	(GLEPE) Mohr, auction 1847, no. 1763.
1047	0·92	14·2	→	—	Ed	o[1]	(GEPPECC) Thomsen 9121.
1048	1·12	17·3	↓	—	G	991	Same obv. die as 1051; same rev. die as 1050. Enner find 1849.
1049	1·04	16·1	→	—	G	cf. 991 (b)	Lübeck find 346.
1050	1·11	17·1	↑	—	G	992	Same rev. die as 1048. No provenance.
1051	1·04	16·1	↑	—	G	993	Same obv. die as 1048. Stockholm 1885.
1052	1·11	17·1	←	—	H	o[1]	Lübeck find 345.
1053	1·10	16·9	←	—	H	o[1]	Same dies. Bruun 270.
1054	0·99	15·3	←	PVLFERD	I	996	Thomsen 9122.
1055	1·15	17·7	←	PVLNOÐ	H	997	Stockholm 1885.
1056	1·15	17·7	←	—	H	997	Same dies. Bruun 271.
1057	1·18	18·2	←	—	H	cf. 997 (b 1)	Store Valby find 1839.
1058	1·13	17·4	↑	PVPERD	I	o	Bolbygaard find 1872.

GOÐABYRH (?)

1059	1·18	18·2	↓	CARLA	E	o	(Rev. trefoil in each quarter.) Kelstrup find 1859.
1060	1·11	17·1	↓	LEOMÆR	I	1000	Bonderup find 1854.
1061	1·10	16·9	↓	—	I	1000	Same dies. Bruun 272.
1062	0·99	15·3	→	PVLFMÆR	E	1001	Stockholm 1885.
1063	0·89	13·7	↑	—	E	cf. 1001	(GOÐ) Same obv. die. Beskrivelse 1791, no. 23. R & D 25. Broken.

GRANTABRICGE (CAMBRIDGE)

| 1064 | 0·97 | 14·9 | ↑ | ADA | E | 1005 | Same obv. die as 1065–6. (T behind neck.) Kelstrup find 1859. |

[1] Moneyer not recorded by Hildebrand for the type.

PLATE 38

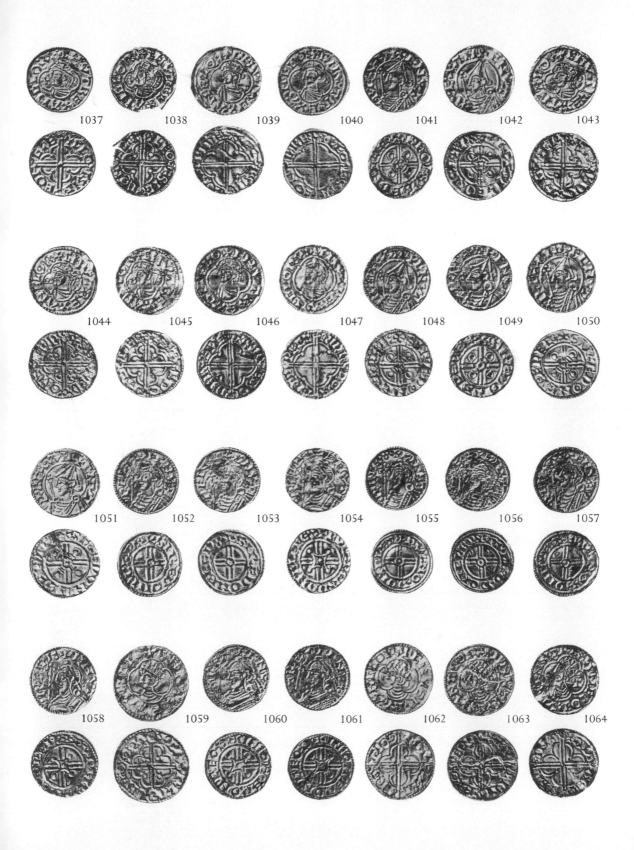

1037 1038 1039 1040 1041 1042 1043

1044 1045 1046 1047 1048 1049 1050

1051 1052 1053 1054 1055 1056 1057

1058 1059 1060 1061 1062 1063 1064

PLATE 39

No.	Weight Gm.	Gr.	Die axis	Moneyer	Hild. type	no.	
CAMBRIDGE (*contd.*)							
1065	0·98	15·1	↓	ADA	E	1005	Same obv. die as 1067 and 1066. Bruun 273, ex Bille-Brahe, ex Thomsen 9123.
1066	1·01	15·6	↓	—	E	1005	Same obv. die as 1064–5. Benzon, donation 1885, no. 16.
1067	(0·86)	(13·2)	↑	—	E	1005	Kelstrup find 1859. Chipped.
1068	1·23	19·0	→	—	G	cf. 1006	Bülow, auction 1827, no. 10. R & D LXII.
1069	0·98	15·1	←	—	G	1007	Lübeck find 346 a.
1070	(1·14)	(17·6)	↑	ADE	E	cf. 1009 (a 9)	Kelstrup find 1859. Chipped.
1071	1·19	18·3	↑	—	E	1011	Same obv. die. Bonderup find 1854.
1072	1·02	15·7	↑	ÆLFÞI	E	1016	Kelstrup find 1859.
1073	1·01	15·6	↑	—	E	1016	Same dies. Bruun 274, ex Bille-Brahe.
1074	1·20	18·5	↓	—	E	o	Pellet in 2 quarters. Kelstrup find 1859.
1075	1·16	17·9	↑	ÆLFÞIG	H	o (cf. 1019)	Kirchhoff 1916.
1076	0·99	15·3	←	ÆLFÞINE	G	o[1]	Lübeck find 348.
1077	0·95	14·6	←	CNIHT	E	1023	Lübeck find 349.
1078	0·93	14·3	←	—	E	cf. 1023	Thomsen 9124.
1079	1·49	23·0	→	—	E	cf. 1023	Enner find 1849.
1080	0·89	13·7	→	CYNIHT	E	1030	Magnus 1868.
1081	0·84	12·9	↗	EADRIC	E	o[1]	Haagerup find 182.
1082	1·20	18·5	↑	EDDÞINE	I	1032	Devegge 1288. Pierced.
1083	1·09	16·8	↑	EDÞINE	H	1034	Bruun 281.
1084	1·21	18·6	→	—	H	1035	Stockholm 1885.
1085	0·91	14·1	→	GODSVNE	I	cf. 1036	Bruun 282.
1086	1·13	17·4	←	GODÞINE	I	1038	R & D Tillæg T. I 30 c.
1087	0·95	14·6	↓	LEOFSI	E	1040	Enner find 1849.
1088	1·12	17·3	→	LEOFSIG	E	1044	Thomsen 9125.
1089	1·38	21·3	↑	LEOFSIGE	E	1046	Bruun 275.
1090	0·92	14·2	←	—	E	1047	Kongsø plantage find 96.
1091	0·98	15·1	↓	—	E	1048	Gartz, auction 1901, no. 1172.
1092	1·07	16·5	↑	—	G	1050	Same dies as 1093. Lübeck find 350.

[1] Moneyer not recorded by Hildebrand for the mint in this reign.

PLATE 39

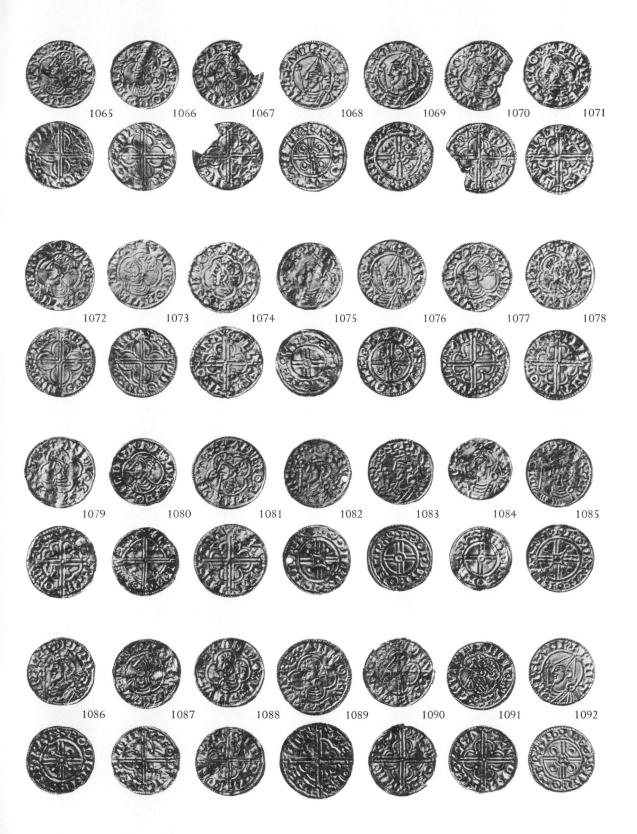

1065 1066 1067 1068 1069 1070 1071

1072 1073 1074 1075 1076 1077 1078

1079 1080 1081 1082 1083 1084 1085

1086 1087 1088 1089 1090 1091 1092

PLATE 40

No.	Weight Gm.	Gr.	Die axis	Moneyer	Hild. type	Hild. no.	

CAMBRIDGE (contd.)

No.	Gm.	Gr.	Die axis	Moneyer	type	no.	Notes
1093	0·81	12·5	↓	LEOFSIGE	G	1050	Same dies as 1092. Bruun 278, ex Bille-Brahe, ex Sorterup, auction 1856, no. 462.
1094	(0·99)	(15·3)	→	LIOFSIG	E	1056	Same obv. die as 1095 and 1099. Kelstrup find 1859. Chipped.
1095	0·84	12·9	→	LIOFSII	E	1057	Same obv. die as 1094 and 1099. Bech, auction 1906, no. 116.
1096	1·06	16·3	→	OREST	G	o[1]	Kelstrup find 1859.
1097	0·80	12·3	↑	—	G	o[1]	Enegaard find 1862.
1098	0·93	14·3	↑	ORIST	E	1061	Hess, auction 1891, no. 938.
1099	0·96	14·8	↑	ORMOST	E	o	Same obv. die as 1094–5. Lübeck find 351.
1100	1·16	17·9	↑	ORNST	E	1062	Lübeck find 352.
1101	1·04	16·1	↑	—	E	1062	Same dies. Bruun 276, ex Bille-Brahe.
1102	0·89	13·7	↓	ORST	E	1064	Lübeck find 353.
1103	0·94	14·5	→	—	E	cf. 1064 (a 7)	Lübeck find 354.
1104	1·09	16·8	↑	—	E	cf. 1064	Same dies. Bruun 277.
1105	0·95	14·6	→	—	E	cf. 1064.	Same dies. Thomsen 9126.
1106	0·85	13·1	→	—	E	cf. 1064	(GRANTB). Stolpehuse find 1837.
1107	0·82	12·6	→	ÞVFSIG	E	o	Kelstrup find 1859.
1108	0·95	14·6	↓	—	E	o	Kelstrup find 1859.
1109	0·94	14·5	←	—	E	o	Same obv. die as 1113. Enner find 1849.
1110	0·88	13·6	↓	ÞVLFSI	E	1066	Kelstrup find 1859.
1111	(1·06)	(16·3)	↓	—	E	1066	Silkeborg Museum 1961. Chipped.
1112	0·92	14·2	→	—	E	1068	Store Valby find 1839.
1113	1·01	15·6	→	—	E	cf. 1068 (a 8)	Same obv. die as 1109. Kirchhoff 1916.
1114	0·83	12·8	→	ÞVLFSIG	E	1071	Benzon, donation 1885, no. 17.
1115	0·93	14·3	↘	—	E	1072	Kelstrup find 1859.
1116	0·90	13·9	↘	—	E	o	Same rev. die. Kelstrup find 1859.
1117	1·29	19·9	↑	ÞVLFSIGE	E	1073	Kelstrup find 1859.
1118	0·88	13·6	←	ÞVLFSII	E	1074	Thomsen 9127.
1119	(0·59)	(9·1)	→	ÞVL(MÆR)	I	cf. 1075	Haagerup find 184. Cut halfpenny.
1120	1·09	16·8	↑	ÞVLSIGE	G	cf. 1077	Same obv. die as 1123; same rev. die as 1122 and 1124. Kongsø plantage find 97.

[1] Moneyer not recorded by Hildebrand for the type.

PLATE 40

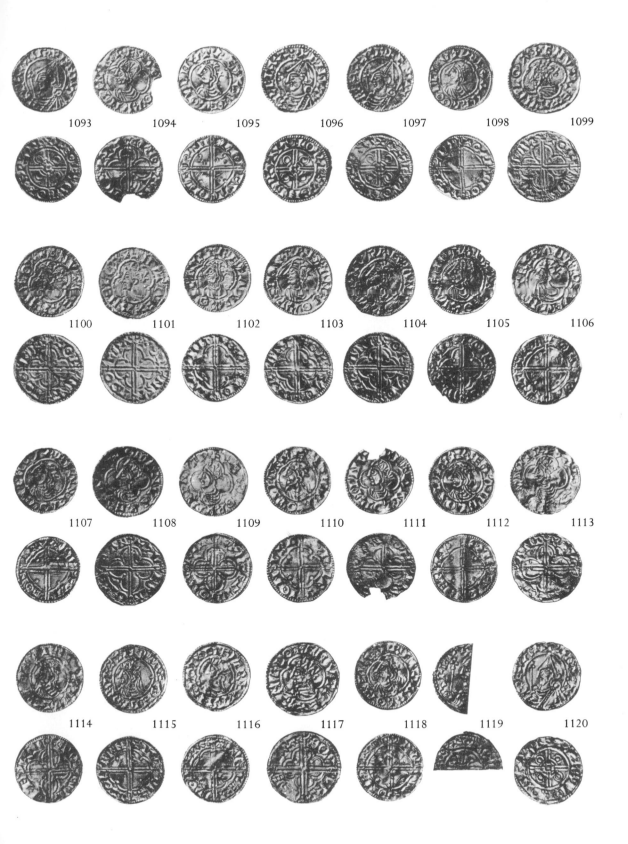

1093 1094 1095 1096 1097 1098 1099

1100 1101 1102 1103 1104 1105 1106

1107 1108 1109 1110 1111 1112 1113

1114 1115 1116 1117 1118 1119 1120

PLATE 41

M

No.	Weight Gm.	Weight Gr.	Die axis	Moneyer	Hild. type	Hild. no.	
CAMBRIDGE (*contd.*)							
1121	1·04	16·1	↑	ᚹVLSIGE	G	cf. 1077	Same obv. die as 1122 and 1124. Bruun 279.
1122	0·95	14·6	←	—	G	cf. 1077	Same dies as 1124; same obv. die as 1121; same rev. die as 1120. Bruun 280, ex Bille-Brahe.
1123	1·14	17·6		—	G	cf. 1077 (a 2)	Same obv. die as 1120. Kelstrup find 1859.
1124	1·19	18·3		—	G	cf. 1077 (b ir. 32, 3)	Same dies as 1122; same obv. die as 1121; same rev. die as 1120. Store Valby find 1839.
GYLDEFORD (GUILDFORD)							
1125	1·14	17·6	↓	ALFᚹOLD	H	o[1]	Bruun 284.
1126	1·11	17·1	↑	BLACAMAN	H	cf. 1079 (b)	R & D Tillæg TI 10a.
1127	1·11	17·1	→	—	H	cf. 1079	Same dies. Bruun 285.
1128	0·96	14·8	→	—	H	1081	Lübeck find 355.
1129	1·03	15·9	←	BLACAMON	H	1082	Same dies as 1130; same rev. die as 1131. Store Valby find 1839.
1130	1·01	15·6	←	—	H	1082	Same dies as 1129; same rev. die as 1131. Bruun 286, ex Bille-Brahe.
1131	1·00	15·4	←	—	H	1083	Same rev. die as 1129–30. Ernst, donation 1964, ex Hauberg, auction 1929, no. 186.
1132	0·98	15·1	↑	SMEAᚹINE	E	o[1]	Bruun 283.
HÆSTINGA (HASTINGS)							
1133	0·83	12·8	→	ÆGELSIGE	G	1087	Lübeck find 357.
1134	0·78	12·1	←	—	G	1087	Same dies. Lübeck find 357.
1135	0·77	11·9	↑	—	G	1087	Same dies. Bruun 288.
1136	0·85	13·1	↓	—	G	cf. 1087 (b)	Lübeck find 356.
1137	0·81	12·5	↓	—	G	cf. 1087	Same dies. Bruun 289, ex Bille-Brahe.
1138	1·04	16·1	↓	ÆLFRD	H	1088	No provenance.
1139	0·81	12·5	↓	ÆLFᚹARD	H	1089	Beskrivelse 1791, no. 12. R & D 32.
1140	0·94	14·5	←	ÆLFᚹEARD	H	cf. 1093	Lübeck find 358.
1141	0·86	13·2	↑	ÆLFᚹERD	E	cf. 1094 (a 6)	Beskrivelse, Tillæg 1794, no. 59. R & D LXVI. Timm, auction 1831, no. 15.
1142	0·92	14·2	→	—	G	1096	Enner find 1849.
1143	1·10	16·9	→	—	G	1097	Kelstrup find 1859.
1144	0·89	13·7	↑	—	G	1098	Lübeck find cf. 363.
1145	0·80	12·3	↓	—	G	1098	Same dies. Benzon, donation 1885, no. 18.
1146	0·85	13·1	→	—	G	1098	Same dies. Bruun 290.
1147	0·85	13·1	↓	—	G	cf. 1098 (b 1)	Store Valby find 1839.
1148	0·82	12·6	→	—	G	cf. 1099 (b 2)	Lübeck find 359.

[1] Moneyer not recorded by Hildebrand for the mint for this reign.

PLATE 41

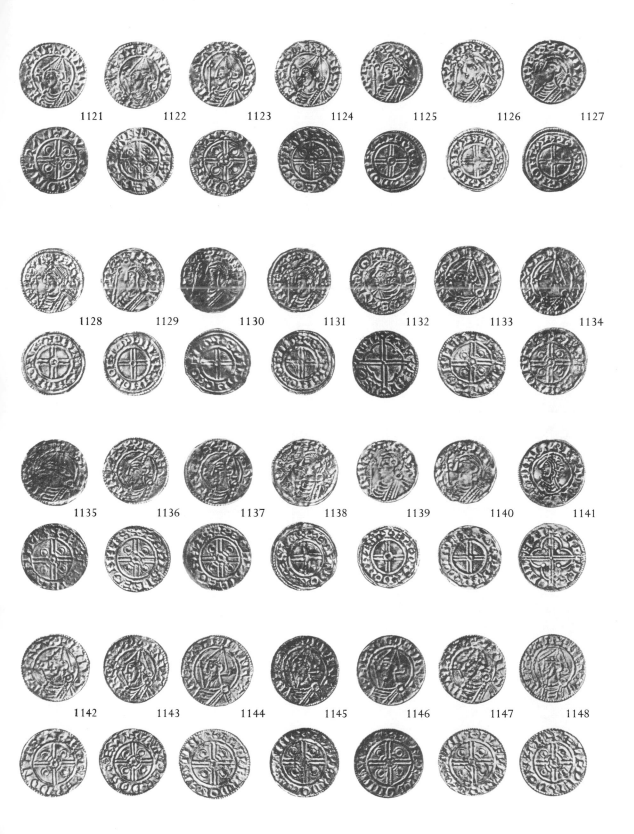

1121   1122   1123   1124   1125   1126   1127

1128   1129   1130   1131   1132   1133   1134

1135   1136   1137   1138   1139   1140   1141

1142   1143   1144   1145   1146   1147   1148

PLATE 42

No.	Weight Gm.	Gr.	Die axis	Moneyer	type	Hild. no.	
HASTINGS (*contd.*)							
1149	1·01	15·6	→	ÆLFÞERD	H	1100	No provenance.
1150	1·10	16·9	→	—	H	1100	Same dies. Bruun 293.
1151	1·00	15·4	↓	—	H	1101	Lübeck find 360.
1152	0·97	14·9	↗	—	H	1102	Same rev. die. Bruun 294, ex Bille-Brahe.
1153	0·84	12·9	↑	ÆLSIG	E	o²	Kelstrup find 1859.
1154	0·99	15·3	→	ÆLSIGE	G	1104	Lübeck find 365.
1155	1·00	15·4	→	—	G	cf. 1104	(HÆSTINI:) Lübeck find 366.
1156	0·80	12·3	←	—	G	cf. 1107	Same dies. Bruun 291, ex Bille-Brahe.
1157	0·95	14·6	←	BRID	H	1105	Lübeck find 367.
1158	1·10	16·9	↑	—	H	o	(HÆSTII) Strøby find 1868.
1159	1·04	16·1	←	—	H	cf. 1105	(HÆSTINC) Same rev. die as 1161. Bruun 295, ex Bille-Brahe.
1160	1·01	15·6	→	—	H	cf. 1105	(HÆSTINC) Bruun 296.
1161	1·01	15·6	←	—	H	o	(HÆSTINC) Same rev. die as 1159. Lübeck find 368.
1162	1·13	17·4	↓	BRIHTNOÐ	G	1109	Lübeck find 384.
1163	0·83	12·8	↑	EADSIIE	G	o	Lübeck find 370.
1164	1·07	16·5	↑	ELSI	E	1111	Bruun 287.
1165	1·08	16·8	↑	ETSIGE	G	1112	Mohr, auction 1847, no. 1766.
1166	1·03	15·9	↓	—	G	cf. 1112 (b)	Lübeck find 372.
1167	0·84	12·9	→	—	G	1113	Lübeck find 375.
1168	0·93	14·3	→	—	G	1113	Same dies. Benzon, donation 1885, no. 19.
1169	0·86	13·2	→	—	G	1113	Same dies. Bruun 292.
1170	1·14	17·6	←	ÞVLNOÐ	H	o¹	Lübeck find 376.
HAMTVNE (NORTHAMPTON OR SOUTHAMPTON)³							
1171	1·14	17·6	↓	ÆLFSIGE	E	cf. 1116 (a 7)	Lübeck find 378.
1172	0·79	12·2	↑	ÆLFÞERD	E	1117	Kelstrup find 1859.
1173	0·96	14·8	→	—	E	1118	Benzon, donation 1885, no. 20.
1174	0·89	13·7	←	—	E	1118	Kirchhoff 1916. Pierced.
1175	0·94	14·5	→	—	E	1120	Enner find 1849.
1176	0·83	12·8	↑	—	E	1120	Bruun 297.

¹ Moneyer **not recorded** by Hildebrand for the mint for this reign.
² Moneyer not recorded by Hildebrand for the type.
³ The probable division of the coins is:
Northampton 1177–86, 1189–99, 1202–6
Southampton 1171–6, 1187–8, 1200–1, 1207–8

PLATE 42

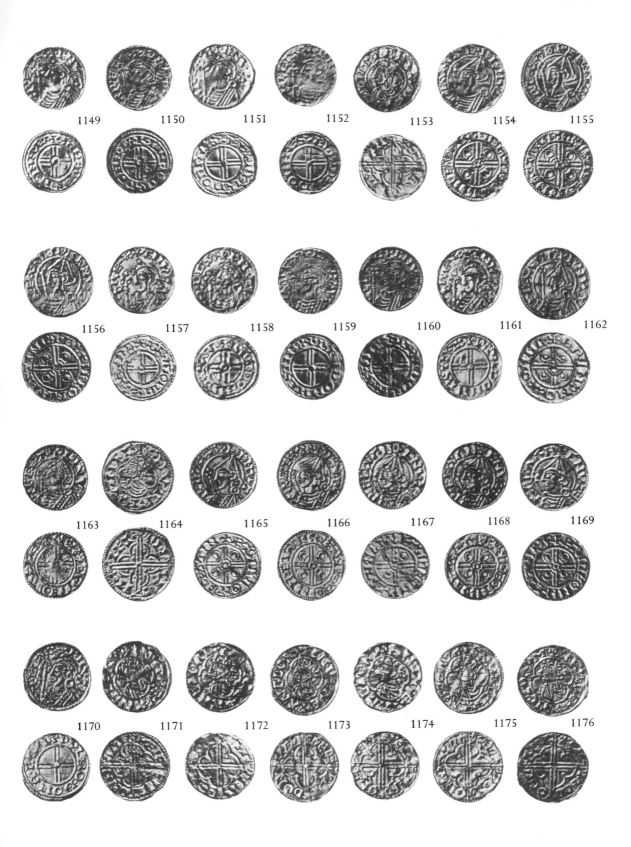

1149 1150 1151 1152 1153 1154 1155

1156 1157 1158 1159 1160 1161 1162

1163 1164 1165 1166 1167 1168 1169

1170 1171 1172 1173 1174 1175 1176

PLATE 43

No.	Weight Gm.	Gr.	Die axis	Moneyer	type	Hild. no.	

NORTHAMPTON OR SOUTHAMPTON (*contd.*)

No.	Gm.	Gr.	Die axis	Moneyer	type	Hild. no.	
1177	1·03	15·9	←	GODRIC	G	1127	Haagerup find 186.
1178	1·03	15·9	←	LEOFNAÐ	E	1129	Same dies as 1179; same obv. die as 1191. Thomsen 9129.
1179	1·06	16·3	↖	—	E	1129	Same dies; same obv. die as 1191. Bruun 298.
1180	0·90	13·9	↓	LEOFNOÐ	E	1130	Kelstrup find 1859.
1181	1·19	18·3	←	—	G	1131	Enner find 1849.
1182	1·14	17·6	←	—	G	1131	Same dies. Bruun 302, ex Bille-Brahe.
1183	0·98	15·1	→	LEOFÞINE	E	o	Kelstrup find 1859.
1184	1·14	17·6	→	—	E	1132	Store Valby find 1839.
1185	1·10	16·9	←	—	E	1132	Same dies. Bruun 299.
1186	1·01	15·6	↙	—	E	1134, rev. 1133	Store Valby find 1839.
1187	0·98	15·1	↑	—	E	1133, rev. 1134	Lübeck find 381.
1188	0·92	14·2	↑	—	E	1133, rev. 1134	Same dies. Kelstrup find 1859.
1189	0·96	14·8	↑	—	E	1136	Same dies as 1190; same rev. die as 1191. Lübeck find (not in *ZfN*).
1190	1·03	15·9	↑	—	E	1136	Same dies as 1189; same rev. die as 1191. Bruun 300.
1191	0·96	14·8	↓	—	E	cf. 1136, obv. 1129	Same obv. die as 1178–9; same rev. die as 1189–90. Store Frigaard find 1928.
1192	0·90	13·9	↓	—	E	1137	Rollin 1856.
1193	0·88	13·6	←	—	E	1137	Same dies. Thomsen 9131.
1194	0·98	15·1	↓	—	G	1139	Store Valby find 1839.
1195	1·07	16·5	↓	—	G	1139	Same dies. Lübeck find 380.
1196	1·26	19·4	↓	—	H	1140	Devegge 1289.
1197	1·13	17·4	↑	—	H	1140	Same dies. Bruun 303.
1198	1·10	16·9	→	—	H	1141	Beskrivelse, Tillæg 1794, p. 9, no. 16. R & D 31.
1199	1·10	16·9	↑	—	H	1141	Same dies. Bruun 304, ex Bille-Brahe, ex Mohr, auction 1847, no. 1767.
1200	0·92	14·2	←	LEOFÞNE	E	1142	Lübeck find cf. 382.
1201	0·86	13·2	↖	—	E	1142	Same dies, Bruun 301.
1202	0·91	14·1	↑	LEOÞOLD	E	cf. 1146 (a 4)	Trefoil and pellets in front of face. Stolpehuse find 1837.
1203	0·86	13·2	→	LIOFÞINE	E	o	Frost, auction 1827, no. 17. R & D LXV.
1204	0·96	14·8	←	—	E	o	Kelstrup find 1859.

PLATE 43

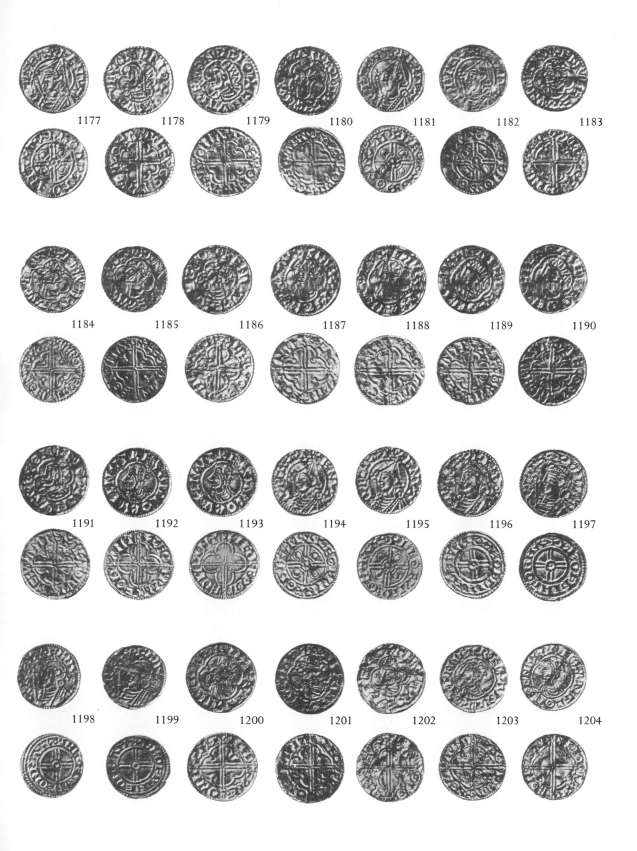

1177 1178 1179 1180 1181 1182 1183

1184 1185 1186 1187 1188 1189 1190

1191 1192 1193 1194 1195 1196 1197

1198 1199 1200 1201 1202 1203 1204

PLATE 44

No.	Weight Gm.	Gr.	Die axis	Moneyer	Hild. type	no.	

NORTHAMPTON OR SOUTHAMPTON (contd.)

No.	Gm.	Gr.	axis	Moneyer	type	no.	
1205	0·94	14·5	→	LIOFꝥINE	E	o	No provenance.
1206	0·93	14·3	←	LIOFꝥOLD	E	cf. 1147	Enner find 1849.
1207	0·98	15·1	←	SIBODA	E	cf. 1148 (a 7)	Lübeck find 383.
1208	1·00	15·4	←	—	E	cf. 1148	Gartz, auction 1901, no. 1174.

HEORTFORD (HERTFORD)

No.	Gm.	Gr.	axis	Moneyer	type	no.	
1209	1·02	15·7	↑	DEORSIE	H	o	Same obv. die as 1210–11. Haagerup find 187.
1210	0·98	15·1	↑	DEORSIGE	H	1150	Same dies as 1211; same obv. die as 1209. Lübeck find 390.
1211	1·05	16·2	→	—	H	1150	Same dies as 1210; same obv. die as 1209. Bruun 309, ex Bille-Brahe.
1212	0·86	13·2	↓	DYRSIG	E	o[1]	Lübeck find 391.
1213	1·07	16·5	↑	DYRSIGE	G	1153	Bruun 308.
1214	0·95	14·6	←	LEOFRIC	H	cf. 1155 (b)	Lübeck find 392.
1215	0·99	15·3	→	—	H	1155	Same obv. die as 1216 and 1218. Bruun 310, ex Bille-Brahe.
1216	1·01	15·6	←	—	H	1156	Same obv. die as 1218; same obv. die as 1215; same rev. die as 1217 and 1219. Lübeck find 394.
1217	0·94	14·5	↑	—	H	cf. 1156	Same obv. die as 1219; same rev. die as 1216 and 1219. Lübeck find 395.
1218	0·98	15·1	↑	—	H	cf. 1156	Same dies as 1216; same obv. die as 1215; same rev. die as 1217 and 1219. Lyngby find 1861. Broken.
1219	0·99	15·3	↑	—	H	cf. 1156	Same dies as 1217; same rev. die as 1216 and 1218. Bruun 311.
1220	1·12	17·3	↓	LEORIC	H	1157	Stolpehuse find 1837.
1221	0·76	11·7	↖	LIFINC	E	1160	Bruun 305.
1222	1·06	16·3	←	—	H	1164	Lübeck find 396.
1505	0·90	13·9	→	LYFINC	E	o	No provenance. (Plate 54.)
1506	1·07	16·5	→	—	E	o	Kelstrup find 1859. (Plate 54.)
1507	1·08	16·6	↓	—	E	o	Thomsen 9305. (Plate 54.)
1508	1·06	16·3	←	—	E	o	Purchased 1856. (Plate 54.)
1223	1·06	16·3	→	—	E	o	Same dies. Bruun 306.
1224	0·84	12·9	←	ꝥVLFRIC	E	cf. 1170 (a 5)	R & D LXIX, Schubart, auction 1831, no. 4.
1225	1·10	16·9	↗	—	E	cf. 1170 (a 5)	Bruun 307.
1226	0·97	14·9	↓	—	E	1176	Enner find 1849.
1227	0·98	15·1	↓	—	E	1178	Same rev. die. Haagerup find 189.
1228	1·30	20·1	→	—	E	1179	Purchased 1886.

HEREFORD (HEREFORD)

No.	Gm.	Gr.	axis	Moneyer	type	no.	
1229	1·16	17·9	↓	ÆLEꝥIG	G	1181	Munksjørup find 1829. R & D Tillæg T. I 33 a.
1230	1·09	16·8	↘	—	G	1181	Same dies. Bruun 315.
1231	1·11	17·1	↓	ELEꝥI	E	o (cf. 1184)	Store Valby find 1839.
1232	1·13	17·4	↓	ELEꝥIG	E	o (cf. 1187)	Gartz, auction 1901, no. 1176.

[1] Moneyer not recorded by Hildebrand for the type.

PLATE 44

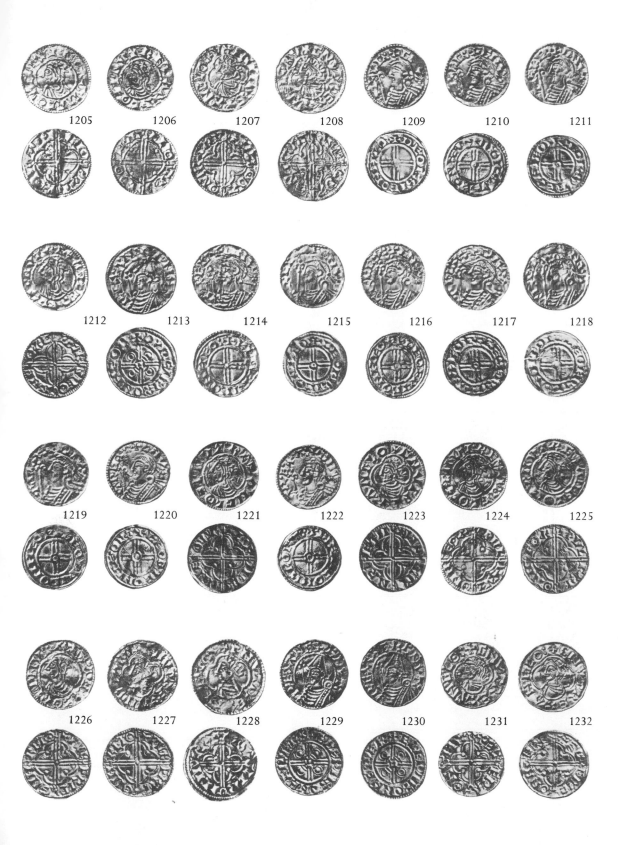

1205 1206 1207 1208 1209 1210 1211

1212 1213 1214 1215 1216 1217 1218

1219 1220 1221 1222 1223 1224 1225

1226 1227 1228 1229 1230 1231 1232

PLATE 45

No.	Weight Gm.	Gr.	Die axis	Moneyer	Hild. type	no.	

HEREFORD (*contd.*)

No.	Gm.	Gr.	Die axis	Moneyer	Hild. type	Hild. no.	
1233	1·10	16·9	↗	ELEÞII	E	cf. 1184	Bruun 312.
1234	1·11	17·1	↓	—	H	o	R & D 33.
1235	0·85	13·1	↑	ETSTAN	Ed	o[1]	Enner find 1849.
1236	1·02	15·7	→	—	G	1190	Same obv. die as 1256. Kelstrup find 1859.
1237	1·12	17·3	↑	—	G	1191	Stolpehuse find 1837.
1238	1·13	17·4	↑	—	H	1194	Gartz, auction 1901, no. 1177.
1239	(0·44)	(6·8)	↙	LE(OFGAR)	E	1196	Bruun 313. Cut halfpenny.
1240	1·14	17·6	→	LEOFGAR	E	1199	Hess, auction 1891, no. 948.
1241	1·10	16·9	→	—	G	cf. 1204	(HER) Siökrona 1883.
1242	1·12	17·3	↓	—	G	cf. 1204	(HERE) Kelstrup find 1859.
1243	1·11	17·1	→	—	G	cf. 1204	Same dies. Bruun 316, ex Bille-Brahe.
1244	1·14	17·6	↑	LEOFENOÐ	I	o[2]	R & D 34.
1245	1·10	16·9	→	LEOFN	H	1205	Glückstadt, auction 1924, no. 43.
1246	1·20	18·5	↓	LEOFNOÐ	H	1207	Petersen, auction 1917, no. 109.
1247	1·13	17·4	↓	—	I	o[2]	Haagerup find 190.
1248	0·92	14·2	↑	ORDRIC	Ed	1208	Enner find 1849.
1249	0·94	14·5	↙	—	Ed	1208	Bruun 314.
1250	1·13	17·4	→	—	G	1210	Same rev. die as 1253. Lübeck find 389.
1251	1·03	15·9	↓	—	G	1211	Same dies as 1252 and 1254. Bülow, auction 1827, no. 14, R & D LXVIII.
1252	1·01	15·6	↑	—	G	1211	Same dies as 1251 and 1254. Thomsen 9135.
1253	1·10	16·9	→	—	G	1211	Same rev. die as 1250. Bruun 317.
1254	1·00	15·4	↑	—	G	1212	Same dies as 1251–2. Bruun 318.
1255	1·15	17·7	↓	—	H	cf. 1213 (b)	Lübeck find 387.
1256	1·12	17·3	←	OÞVLSIGE	G	1214	Same obv. die as 1236. Enegaard find 1862.
1257	(0·45)	(6·9)	←	ÞVL(SIGE)	Ed	1216	Ernst, donation 1964, [ex Hauberg, auction 1929, no. 435. Cut halfpenny.
1258	1·13	17·4	←	ÞVLSIGE	H	1218	Stockholm 1885.

HVNTANDVNE (HUNTINGDON)

No.	Gm.	Gr.	Die axis	Moneyer	Hild. type	Hild. no.	
1259	1·14	17·6	↑	ADA	H	1219	Same rev. die as 1260–1. Lübeck find 397.
1260	1·11	17·1	←	—	H	1219	Same dies as 1261; same rev. die as 1259. Stockholm 1885.

[1] Moneyer not recorded by Hildebrand for the type.
[2] Moneyer not recorded by Hildebrand for the type in name of Cnut.

PLATE 45

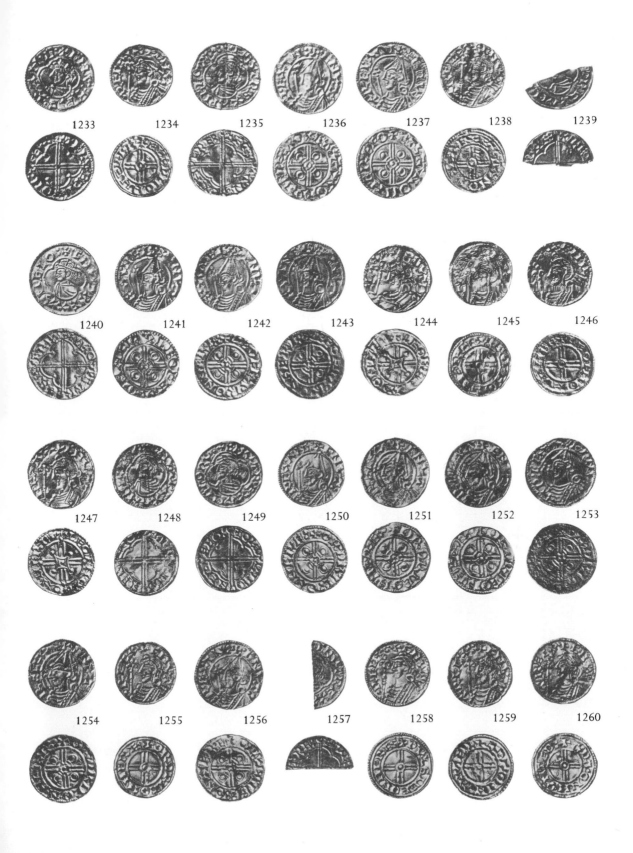

1233   1234   1235   1236   1237   1238   1239

1240   1241   1242   1243   1244   1245   1246

1247   1248   1249   1250   1251   1252   1253

1254   1255   1256   1257   1258   1259   1260

PLATE 46

No.	Weight Gm.	Gr.	Die axis	Moneyer	Hild type	Hild no.	

HUNTINGDON (*contd.*)

No.	Gm.	Gr.	axis	Moneyer	type	no.	
1261	1·10	16·9	→	ADA	H	1219	Same dies as 1260; same rev. die as 1259. Bruun 324, ex Bille-Brahe.
1262	1·05	16·2	↓	ÆADNOÐ	G	1221	R & D LXX. Thomsen 9137.
1263	1·05	16·2	←	—	G	1221	Same dies. Bruun 320, ex Bille-Brahe.
1264	1·11	17·1	↑	ÆLFGAR	H	o[1]	R & D Tillæg T. I. 34c.
1265	1·09	16·8	→	—	H	o[1]	Same dies. Bruun 325.
1266	0·96	14·8	→	EADNOÐ	E	o	Same obv. die as 1271. Enner find 1849.
1267	1·09	16·8	←	—	G	1232	Lübeck find 399.
1268	1·06	16·3	↑	—	G	1233	Lübeck find 400.
1269	1·05	16·2	↓	EDNOD	E	cf. 1236 (a 7)	Lübeck find 402.
1270	1·26	19·4	↘	—	E	cf. 1236 (a 10)	Bruun 319.
1271	0·95	14·6	→	—	E	o	Same obv. die as 1266. Enner find 1849.
1272	1·09	16·8	↑	FÆRÐEN	E	1238	Kelstrup find 1859.
1273	1·01	15·6	↑	GODELAÐ	G	1239	Kelstrup find 1859.
1274	1·02	15·7	↓	—	G	1239	Same dies. Bruun 321, ex Bille-Brahe.
1275	0·89	13·7	↓	GODELEOE	G	1241	Ernst, donation 1964. Cracked.
1276	1·02	15·7	↑	GODELEOF	G	1244	Store Valby find 1839.
1277	1·05	16·2	↑	—	G	1244	Same dies. Bruun 322.
1278	0·89	13·7	→	—	G	cf. 1244	(HVT) Kelstrup find 1859.
1279	1·07	16·5	↓	—	G	1246	Kelstrup find 1859.
1280	0·98	15·1	→	—	G	1246	Same rev. die. Haagerup find 191.
1281	1·00	15·4	↓	GODLEOF	E	1249	R & D Tillæg T. I. 34d.
1282	1·04	16·1	←	—	G	1251	Thomsen 9138.
1283	0·88	13·6	←	GODLIOF	E	o	Lübeck find 406.
1284	0·98	15·1	→	—	G	o	R & D 35. Pierced.
1285	1·02	15·7	→	—	G	o	Same dies. Bruun 323, ex Bille-Brahe, ex Mohr, auction 1847, no. 1770.
1286	1·01	15·6	↓	—	G	o	Same rev. die. Munksjørup find 1829.
1287	0·88	13·6	→	GOFRIC	G	o[1]	Lübeck find 407.
1288	0·85	13·1	←	SÆÞINE	E	o[1]	Enner find 1849.

[1] Moneyer not recorded by Hildebrand for the mint for this reign.

PLATE 46

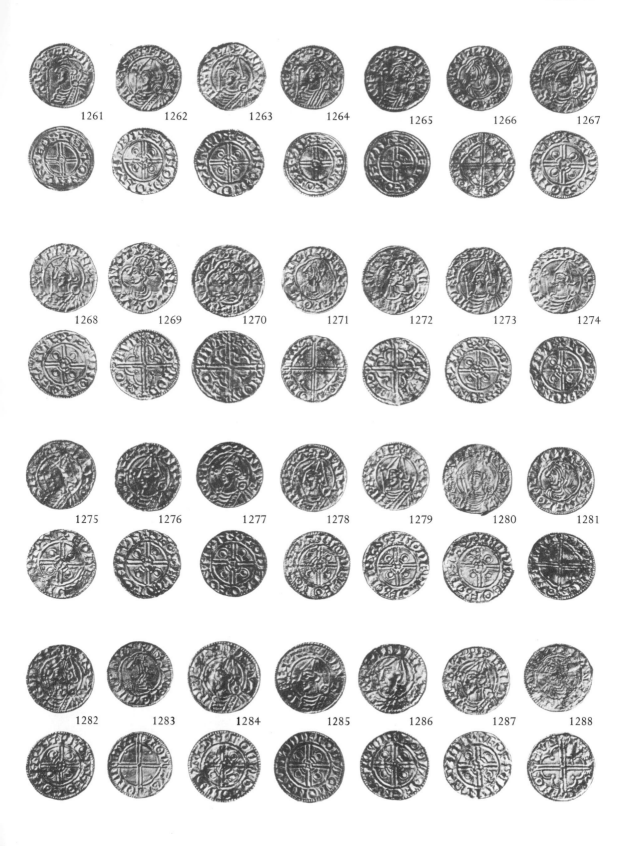

1261 1262 1263 1264 1265 1266 1267

1268 1269 1270 1271 1272 1273 1274

1275 1276 1277 1278 1279 1280 1281

1282 1283 1284 1285 1286 1287 1288

PLATE 47

No.	Weight Gm.	Gr.	Die axis	Moneyer	Hild. type	Hild. no.	
HUNTINGDON (contd.)							
1289	0·82	12·6	→	ꝶVLFꝶINE	H	o[1]	Kongsø plantage find 98.
1290	0·84	12·9	→	—	H	o[1]	Bruun 326.
1291	1·10	16·9	↓	ꝶVLSTAN	I	o[2]	Bruun 327.
LANGPORT (LANGPORT)							
1292	1·13	17·4	↑	ÆGELꝶINE	H	o[3]	R & D LXXIII. Frost, auction 1827, no. 18.
1293	0·85	13·1	←	ÆLFSIG	E	o[1]	Kelstrup find 1859.
1294	0·91	14·1	↓	—	E	o[1]	Same obv. die as Hild. 881 of Ilchester (see *BNJ* xxix, pp. 65–6). Kelstrup find 1859.
1295	0·95	14·6	↑	EDRIC	G	o[3]	*BMC* 266. Stolpehuse find 1837.
1296	0·88	13·6	↓	—	G	o[3]	Same dies. Bruun 337.
1297	1·00	15·4	←	GODꝶINE	E	o	*BMC* 265. Store Frigaard find 1928.
1298							See Canterbury, pl. 6.
LÆꝶES (LEWES)							
1299	1·12	17·3	↑	ÆLFꝶERD	G	1257	Stockholm 1885.
1300	1·00	15·4	←	—	G	1257	Lübeck find 415.
1301	1·10	16·9	→	—	H	1258	Lübeck find 413.
1302	1·17	18·1	↓	—	H	o	Lübeck find 414.
1303	1·14	17·6	↑	ÆLFꝶERDD	G	1259	Lübeck find 415 a.
1304	1·00	15·4	←	—	G	cf. 1259 (b 1)	Benzon, donation 1885, no. 21.
1305	1·04	16·1	→	ÆLFꝶINE	E	o[1]	Stolpehuse find 1837.
1306	0·81	12·5	↓	COLLINI	G	1263	Beskrivelse, Tillæg 1794, no. 9. R & D 50. Chipped.
1307	0·98	15·1	→	EADꝶINE	G	1264	Lübeck find 416.
1308	0·95	14·6	→	—	G	1264	Same dies. Bruun 331, ex Bille-Brahe.
1309	0·92	14·2	→	EALDRED	E	1265	Enner find 1849.
1310	0·99	15·3	←	EDꝶARD	I	1267	Same rev. die as 1314–15. Bruun 335.
1311	1·22	18·8	↓	EDꝶINE	H	1268	Same rev. die as 1314–15. Haagerup find 193.
1312	1·16	17·9	↓	—	H	1269	Same dies as 1313; same obv. die as 1314–15. Thomsen 9139.
1313	1·05	16·2	↓	—	H	1269	Same dies as 1312; same obv. die as 1314–15. Bruun 333.
1314	1·12	17·3	→	—	H	1269	Same dies as 1315; same obv. die as 1312–13; same rev. die as 1311. Ernst, donation 1964.
1315	1·12	17·3	↑	—	H	1270	Same dies as 1315; same obv. die as 1312–13; same rev. die as 1311. Bruun 334, ex Bille-Brahe.
1316	1·10	16·9	←	—	I	1271	Same dies as 1317. Haagerup find 194.

[1] Moneyer not recorded by Hildebrand for the mint in this reign.
[2] Moneyer not recorded by Hildebrand for the type.
[3] Moneyer not recorded for moneyer or type at this mint in this reign.

PLATE 47

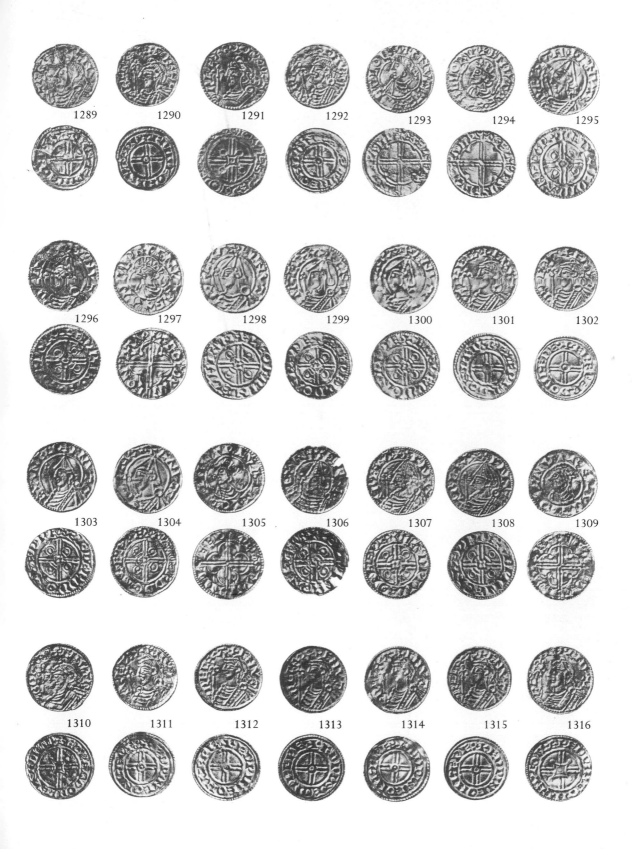

1289 1290 1291 1292 1293 1294 1295

1296 1297 1298 1299 1300 1301 1302

1303 1304 1305 1306 1307 1308 1309

1310 1311 1312 1313 1314 1315 1316

PLATE 48

No.	Weight Gm.	Gr.	Die axis	Moneyer	type	Hild. no.	

LEWES (contd.)

No.	Gm.	Gr.	Die axis	Moneyer	type	Hild. no.	Notes
1317	1·07	16·5	↓	EDÞINE	I	1271	Same dies as 1316. Bruun 336.
1318	1·00	15·4	→	GODEFRIÐ	G	1272	Enner find 1849,
1319	1·04	16·1	↑	—	G	1272	Same rev. die as 1321. Bruun 332.
1320	1·13	17·4	→	—	G	1273	Stockholm 1885.
1321	1·16	17·9	←	—	G	o	Same obv. die as 1322; same rev. die as 1319. Enner find 1849.
1322	1·15	17·7	↑	—	G	o	Same obv. die as 1321. Lübeck find 418.
1323	(0·56)	(8·7)	→	—	H	1278	Kirke Værløse find 186. Cut halfpenny.
1324	0·95	14·6	↙	GODEMAN	E	1278	Bruun 328.
1325	1·29	19·9	←	GODMAN	E	cf. 1279	Kelstrup find 1859.
1326	0·83	12·8	→	—	E	cf. 1279	Lübeck find 418 a (sic!).
1327	1·01	15·6	←	GODÞI	E	1339	Store Valby find 1839.
1328	1·11	17·1	↓	LEEFA	E	1281	Enner find 1849.
1329	1·12	17·3	↓	—	E	1281	Same obv. die. Bruun 329, ex Bille-Brahe, ex Thomsen 9140.
1330	1·33	20·6	→	LEFA	Ea	o	Beskrivelse 1791, no. 29. R & D 49.
1331	1·46	22·5	↖	—	Ea	o	Same dies. Bruun 330.
1332	1·46	22·5	←	LEOFNOD	E	o[1]	Gartz, auction 1901, no. 1178.
1333	0·89	13·7	←	LEOFÞIN	E	o	Lübeck find (not in ZfN).
1334	1·21	18·7	→	LEOFÞINE	E	1284	Enner find 1849.
1335	0·97	14·9	→	—	E	o	Enner find 1849.
1336	1·26	19·4	↑	LEOFÞNE	E	o	Kelstrup find 1859.
1337	1·12	17·3	→	NORÐMAN	I	1287	Haagerup find 195.

LEIGCEASTER (CHESTER)

No.	Gm.	Gr.	Die axis	Moneyer	type	Hild. no.	Notes
1338	1·05	16·2	↑	ÆLFNOÐ	E	1291	Lyngby find 1861.
1339	1·09	16·8	↑	—	G	1293	No provenance.
1340	1·11	17·1	↓	—	G	1294	Enner find 1849.
1341	1·03	15·9	↑	—	G	1294	Bruun 351, ex Bille-Brahe.
1342	1·19	18·3	↑	—	G	cf. 1294 (a 1)	Lübeck find 428.
1343	1·01	15·6	↓	—	G	cf. 1294	Bruun 352.
1344	1·14	17·6	→	—	G	cf. 1294	Enner find 1849.

[1] Moneyer not recorded by Hildebrand for the mint in this reign.

PLATE 48

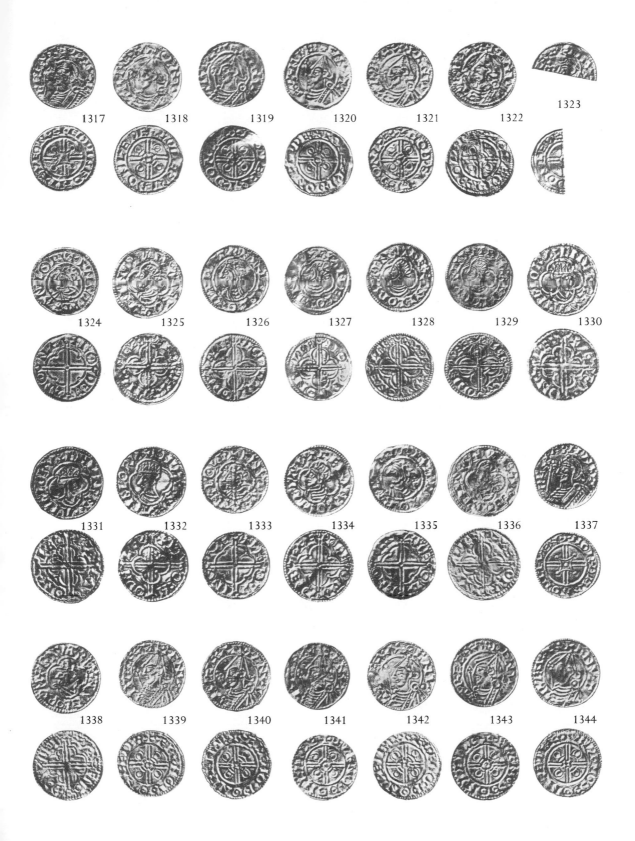

1317   1318   1319   1320   1321   1322

1323

1324   1325   1326   1327   1328   1329   1330

1331   1332   1333   1334   1335   1336   1337

1338   1339   1340   1341   1342   1343   1344

PLATE 49

O

No.	Weight Gm.	Gr.	Die axis	Moneyer	Hild. type	no.	
CHESTER (contd.)							
1345	1·11	17·1	→	ÆLFNOÐ	H	1295	Thomsen 9141.
1346	1·05	16·2	←	ÆLFSI	E	1298	Gartz, auction 1901, no. 1179.
1347	1·14	17·6	↑	ÆLFSIE	H	o	Lübeck find 430.
1348	0·75	11·5	↑	ÆLFSIG	E	o	Kelstrup find 1859.
1349	1·23	19·0	↑	ÆLFSIGE	G	1302	Enner find 1849.
1350	1·11	17·1	←	—	G	1302	Same obv. die. Bruun 353, ex Bille-Brahe.
1351	1·03	15·9	↑	—	H	1303	Hauberg, auction 1929, no. 208.
1352	1·17	18·1	→	—	H	1304	Kirchhoff 1916.
1353	1·10	16·9	→	—	H	1304	Bruun 367.
1354	1·14	17·6	→	—	H	1305	Lübeck find 432.
1355	1·08	16·6	→	—	H	1306	Lübeck find 433.
1356	1·12	17·3	→	ÆLNOÐ	H	1308	Lübeck find 434.
1357	1·70	26·2	↑	ÆÐERIC	E	1312	Kelstrup find 1859.
1358	1·03	15·9	←	—	E	cf. 1312	Kelstrup find 1859.
1359	1·36	21·0	←	—	E	cf. 1312	Kelstrup find 1859.
1360	0·94	14·5	←	ÆÐRIC	E	o (cf. 1313)	Beskrivelse, Tillæg 1794, no. 27. R & D 40.
1361	0·93	14·3	↑	ALCSI	E	cf. 1315	Haagerup find 196.
1362	1·11	17·1	←	BRVNNINC	I	o[1]	Thomsen 9142.
1363	1·05	16·2	←	CEOLNAÐ	E	cf. 1316	Enner find 1849.
1364	0·98	15·1	↘	—	E	cf. 1316	Bruun 338. Pierced.
1365	0·95	14·6	→	CEOLNOÐ	E	1317	Kelstrup find 1859.
1366	1·09	16·8	←	—	E	cf. 1317	Kelstrup find 1859.
1367	1·07	16·5	←	—	E	cf. 1317	Same rev. die. Bruun 339, ex Bille-Brahe.
1368	1·12	17·3	→	—	E	1319	Store Valby find 1839.
1369	1·09	16·8	↑	—	G	cf. 1320	Lübeck find 435.
1370	1·16	17·9	↑	—	G	1320	Bruun 354, ex Bille-Brahe, ex Sorterup, auction 1856, no. 464.
1371	1·15	17·7	↑	—	G	cf. 1320 (a 2)	Lübeck find 437.
1372	0·81	12·5	←	'CLHOE'	H	o	(? Ælnoth cf. 1356.) Gartz, auction 1901, no. 1180 (Hild. 1308).

[1] Moneyer not recorded by Hildebrand for the mint in the name of Cnut or Harthacnut.

PLATE 49

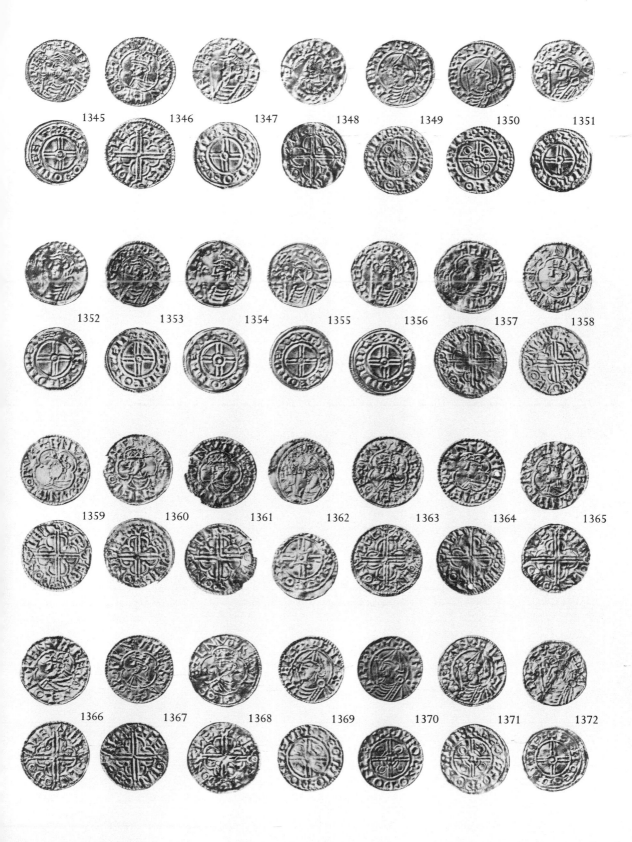

1345 1346 1347 1348 1349 1350 1351

1352 1353 1354 1355 1356 1357 1358

1359 1360 1361 1362 1363 1364 1365

1366 1367 1368 1369 1370 1371 1372

PLATE 50

No.	Weight Gm.	Gr.	Die axis	Moneyer	Hild. type	no.	
CHESTER (contd.)							
1373	1·09	16·8	↓	CROC	E	1322	Stockholm 1854.
1374	1·01	15·6	↓	—	E	1322	Same dies. Bruun 340, ex Bille-Brahe, ex Thomsen 9144.
1375	0·78	12·1	↑	—	G	1323	Enner find 1849.
1376	0·99	15·3	→	—	G	1323	Bruun 355, ex Bille-Brahe, ex Sorterup, auction 1856, no. 465.
1377	1·00	15·4	↓	EELNAÐ	E	0	Enner find 1849.
1378	1·02	15·7	→	ELEÞINE	E	cf. 1328	Bust flanked by trefoils. Lübeck find 438 a.
1379	1·07	16·5	↓	—	E	1328	Store Valby find 1839.
1380	1·10	16·9	↓	—	E	1330	Bruun 341, ex Bille-Brahe.
1381	1·22	18·8	↙	—	E	1330	Same dies. Kelstrup find 1859.
1382	1·11	17·1	↑	—	G	1332	Store Valby find 1839.
1383	1·13	17·4	→	—	G	1332	Same dies. Bruun 356, ex Bille-Brahe.
1384	1·03	15·9	↓	—	G	1333	Lübeck find 439.
1385	1·17	18·1	↑	—	H	1335	R & D 36.
1386	1·11	17·1	←	—	H	1337	Stockholm 1885.
1387	1·10	16·9	↓	'ETEÞERD'	E	0[1]	Lübeck find (not in *ZfN*).
1388	1·08	16·6	←	GODÞINE	E	1340	Beskrivelse, Tillæg 1794, no. 20. R & D 41.
1389	1·09	16·8	↙	—	E	1340	Bruun 342, ex Bille-Brahe, ex Stockholm 1854.
1390	1·02	15·7	↑	—	E	cf. 1340	Curt, London 1858.
1391	0·76	11·7	→	—	E	1345	Thomsen 9147. Cracked.
1392	1·05	16·2	→	—	E	1347	Lübeck find (not in *ZfN*).
1393	(0·90)	(13·9)	↙	—	E	cf. 1347	Sankt Jørgensbjerg find 8. Chipped.
1394	1·05	16·2	←	—	G	cf. 1349	Beskrivelse, Tillæg 1794, no. 10. R & D 37.
1395	0·94	14·5	↑	—	G	cf. 1349	Same dies. Bruun 357, ex Bille-Brahe.
1396	1·04	16·1	←	—	G	1350	Stockholm 1861.
1397	1·04	16·1	↑	—	G	1350	Same rev. die. Stockholm 1885.
1398	0·98	15·1	↑	GUNLEF	E	cf. 1352	Beskrivelse, Tillæg 1794, no. 26. R & D 42.
1399	0·86	13·2	↑	—	E	cf. 1352	Thomsen 9148.
1400	1·05	16·2	→	GUNLEOF	E	cf. 1353	(LE). Purchased 1858.

[1] Moneyer not recorded by Hildebrand for the type.

PLATE 50

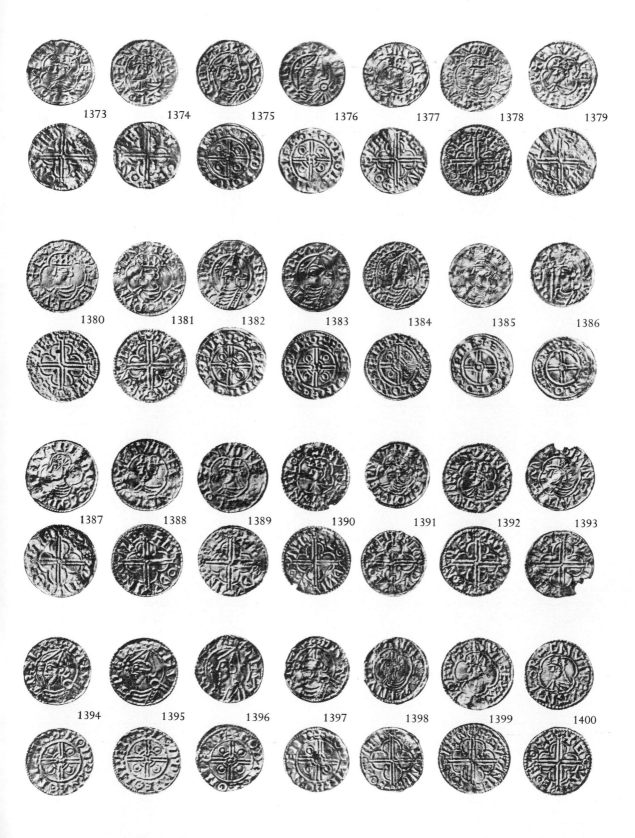

1373   1374   1375   1376   1377   1378   1379

1380   1381   1382   1383   1384   1385   1386

1387   1388   1389   1390   1391   1392   1393

1394   1395   1396   1397   1398   1399   1400

PLATE 51

No.	Weight Gm.	Weight Gr.	Die axis	Moneyer	Hild. type	Hild. no.	
CHESTER (contd.)							
1401	1·35	20·8	→	GUNLEOF	E	1352	R & D 43.
1402	1·00	15·4	↓	—	E	1352	Bruun 343, ex Bille-Brahe, ex Stockholm 1854.
1403	1·09	16·8	↑	—	H	cf. 1355 (b)	Lübeck find 441.
1404	0·95	14·6	→	LEFNOÐ	G	o	Store Valby find 1839.
1405	1·06	16·3	↓	LEOFA	E	cf. 1358	(LE) Curt, London 1858.
1406	1·38	21·3	↑	—	E	1356	Kelstrup find 1859.
1407	1·07	16·5	←	—	E	cf. 1358 (a 6)	Kelstrup find 1859. Broken.
1408	1·14	17·6	↓	LEOFENOÐ	E	1361	Same dies as 1410. Stockholm 1854.
1409	0·98	15·1	→	—	E	1361	Sankt Jørgensbjerg find 9. Broken.
1410	1·28	19·7	↖	—	E	1361	Same dies as 1408. Bruun 344, ex Bille-Brahe, ex Thomsen 9149.
1411	1·03	15·9	↑	LEOFIC	E	1362	Lübeck find 458.
1412	0·91	14·1	→	—	E	cf. 1362	(LEI) Same dies. Bonderup find 1854.
1413	0·96	14·8	↓	LEOFN	E	o	Store Valby find 1839, or Enner find 1849.
1414	1·14	17·6	↓	LEOFNOÐ	G	1366	Enner find 1849.
1415	1·14	17·6	↓	—	G	1366	Bruun 358, ex Kongsø plantage find 100.
1416	1·00	15·4	↑	—	G	1368	Stockholm 1885.
1417	0·99	15·3	↑	—	G	1370	Thomsen 9154.
1418	0·88	13·6	←	LEOFS	E	1371	Kelstrup find 1859.
1419	0·78	12·1	↓	—	E	1371	Same dies. Bruun 345.
1420	1·04	16·1	←	LEOFSI	E	cf. 1373	Kelstrup find 1859.
1421	1·05	16·2	↖	—	E	cf. 1373	Bruun 346.
1422	1·08	16·6	↑	LEOFSIGE	G	1376	Beskrivelse 1791, no. 4. R & D 38.
1423	1·14	17·6	↑	—	H	cf. 1378	Same dies as 1425. Lübeck find 444.
1424	1·13	17·4	↓	—	H	1379	Bruun 368, ex Bille-Brahe.
1425	1·13	17·4	←	—	H	1378	Same dies as 1423. Bruun 369.
1426	0·96	14·8	↑	LEOFSIGIGE	G	1380	Bruun 359.
1427	1·28	19·7	↓	LEOFƿI	E	1381	Beskrivelse, Tillæg 1794, no. 41. R & D 45.
1428	1·08	16·6	↖	—	E	1381	Same dies. Bruun 347.

Plate 51

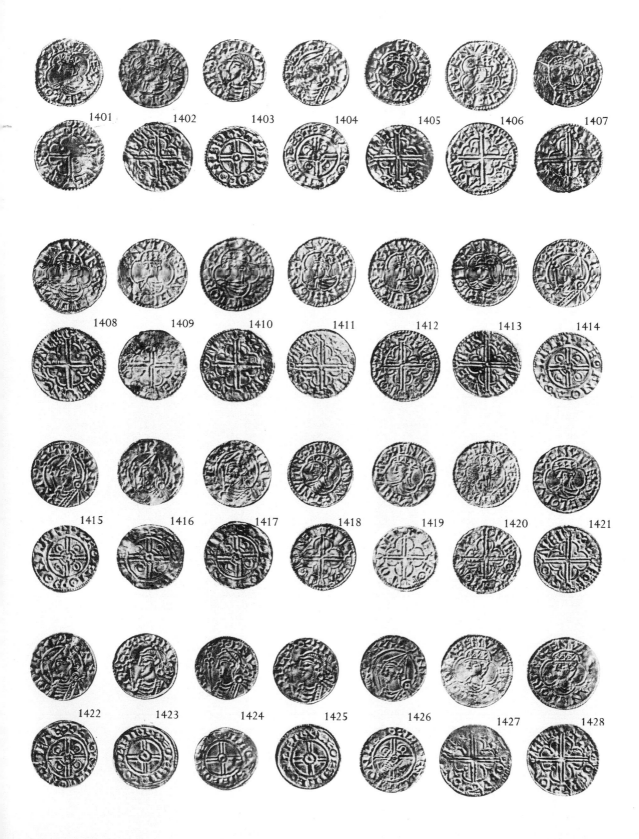

1401 1402 1403 1404 1405 1406 1407

1408 1409 1410 1411 1412 1413 1414

1415 1416 1417 1418 1419 1420 1421

1422 1423 1424 1425 1426 1427 1428

PLATE 52

No.	Weight Gm.	Gr.	Die axis	Moneyer	Hild. type	no.	
CHESTER (*contd.*)							
1429	1·00	15·4	↑	LEOFᵽIG	G	1384	Same dies as 1431; same rev. die as 1430. R & D LXXV. Frost, auction 1827, no. 21, Schubart, auction 1831, no. 5.
1430	1·02	15·8	→	—	G	1384	Same obv. die as 1438; same rev. die as 1429 and 1431. Bruun 360.
1431	1·00	15·4	←	—	G	1384	Same dies as 1429; same rev. die as 1430. Bruun 361, ex Bille-Brahe.
1432	1·12	17·3	↓	—	G	o	Lübeck find 442.
1433	1·01	15·6	↓	—	G	o	Lübeck find 459.
1434	0·83	12·8	→	LEOFᵽIN	G	o	Lübeck find 460.
1435	1·29	19·9	→	LEOFᵽINE	E	1388	Benzon, donation 1885, no. 23.
1436	0·95	14·6	↑	—	E	cf. 1388	Lübeck find 443.
1437	1·14	17·6	↑	—	G	1390	Same rev. die as 1439–41. Bruun 362.
1438	1·01	15·6	→	—	G	1391	Same obv. die as 1430. No provenance.
1439	1·15	17·7	→	—	G	1391	Same rev. die as 1437 and 1440–1. Bruun 363.
1440	1·14	17·6	↓	—	G	1392	Same dies as 1441; same rev. die as 1437 and 1439. Store Valby find 1839 or Enner find 1849.
1441	1·09	16·8	←	—	G	1392	Same dies as 1440; same rev. die as 1437 and 1439. Bruun 364, ex Bille-Brahe.
1442	1·11	17·1	↑	—	H	cf. 1396	(LEGII:) Lübeck find 462.
1443	1·08	16·6	←	—	H	cf. 1396	Same dies. Bruun 370, ex Bille-Brahe.
1444	1·10	16·9	←	—	H	o	(LEI) Lübeck find 446.
1445	0·78	12·1	←	LEONENE	E	1397	Beskrivelse 1791, no. 17. R & D 44.
1446	0·92	14·2	↑	LEONOÐ	E	1399/1398	Curt, London 1858.
1447	1·06	16·3	↓	LEOᵽI	E	1403	Lyngby find 1861.
1448	1·05	16·2	↑	LEOᵽINE	E	1407	R & D 46.
1449	1·02	15·7	↓	LIFIG	E	1409	Lübeck find 463.
1450	1·07	16·5	←	LIFINC	G	1411	Same dies as 1451; same rev. die as 1453. Lübeck find 449.
1451	1·12	17·3	←	—	G	1411	Same dies as 1450; same rev. die as 1453. Bruun 365.
1452	0·86	13·2	←	—	G	1412	Enner find 1849.
1453	0·97	14·9	↑	—	G	1412	Same rev. die as 1450–1. Store Valby find 1839.
1454	0·85	13·1	↑	LIᵽINE	E	1414	Thomsen 9150.
1455	1·00	15·4	←	—	E	1414	Bruun 348, ex Bille-Brahe, ex Mohr, auction 1847, no. 1774.
1456	0·94	15·5	↖	MACSUÐA	E	o (cf. 1416)	Haagerup find 197.

PLATE 52

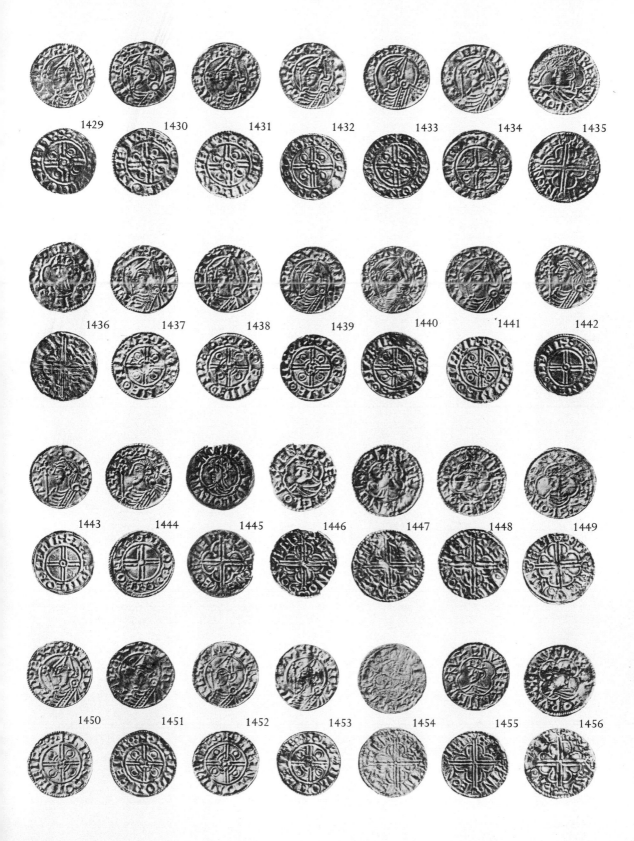

1429   1430   1431   1432   1433   1434   1435

1436   1437   1438   1439   1440   1441   1442

1443   1444   1445   1446   1447   1448   1449

1450   1451   1452   1453   1454   1455   1456

PLATE 53

No.	Weight Gm.	Gr.	Die axis	Moneyer	type	Hild. no.	
CHESTER (*contd.*)							
1457	(0·54)	(8·3)	→	(MA)CSVÐAN	E	1416	Cut halfpenny. Ernst, donation 1964, ex Hauberg, auction 1929, no. 435.
1458	0·96	14·8	←	SNEL	E	cf. 1417	(ANGNLOR) Gartz, auction 1901, no. 1181.
1459	1·08	16·6	↙	—	E	1418	No provenance.
1460	1·04	16·1	→	—	E	1418	Same dies. Bruun 349.
1461	(0·80)	(12·4)	↖	SNE..ARHASNEL	G	0[1]	Beskrivelse, Tillæg 1794, no. 8, R & D 39. Chipped.
1462	1·01	15·6	↓	SPARTIC	E	1424	Kelstrup find 1859.
1463	1·21	18·6	→	SPARTIN	E	0	Bonderup find 1854.
1464	1·12	17·3	→	SPEARTINC	G	1428	Lyngby find 1861.
1465	1·13	17·4	↖	SPEGEN	E	0 (cf. 1430)	Beskrivelse, Tillæg 1794, no. 24. R & D 47.
1466	1·02	15·7	→	SPEGN	E	1430	Kelstrup find 1859.
1467	1·01	15·6	→	TROTAN	E	1432	Enner find 1849.
1468	1·02	15·7	↖	—	E	1432	Bruun 350.
1469	1·17	18·1	→	—	E	cf. 1432 (a 7)	Beskrivelse, Tillæg 1794, no. 22. R & D 48.
1470	1·00	15·4	→	—	E	cf. 1432	(LEI) Lübeck find 466.
1471	1·04	16·1	↓	—	G	1433	Lübeck find 450.
1472	1·06	16·3	←	PVLSI	E	1436	Kelstrup find 1859.
1473	0·92	14·2	↓	LILOSIE	E	0	Kelstrup find 1859.
LEHERCEASTER (LEICESTER)							
1474	1·04	16·1	→	ÆGELPIG	G	1440	Same obv. die as 1476. Lübeck find 452.
1475	1·12	17·3	←	—	H	0[2]	Bruun 375.
1476	1·06	16·3	↑	ÆGELPINE	G	1441	Same obv. die as 1474; same rev. die as 1477. Enner find 1849.
1477	1·10	16·9	↑	—	G	1441	Same rev. die as 1476. Lübeck find 453.
1478	1·15	17·7	←	—	G	cf. 1441	Bruun 374, ex Bille-Brahe, ex Siökrona 1883.
1479	0·92	14·2	↑	ÆLFPI	E	1442	No provenance.
1480	1·28	19·7	←	—	E	1443	Store Valby find 1839.
1481	1·05	16·2	→	ÆLFPII	E	0	Kelstrup find 1859.
1482	0·96	14·8	←	ÆÐELPI	E	1445	Stockholm 1861.
1483	1·03	15·9	↓	—	E	1445	Bruun 371, ex Bille-Brahe. Cracked.
1484	1·07	16·5	↓	—	E	1445	Same dies. Lübeck find 456.

[1] This (? compound) name, Snelcar Hasnel?, not recorded by Hildebrand for the mint in this reign.
[2] Moneyer not recorded by Hildebrand for the type.

PLATE 53

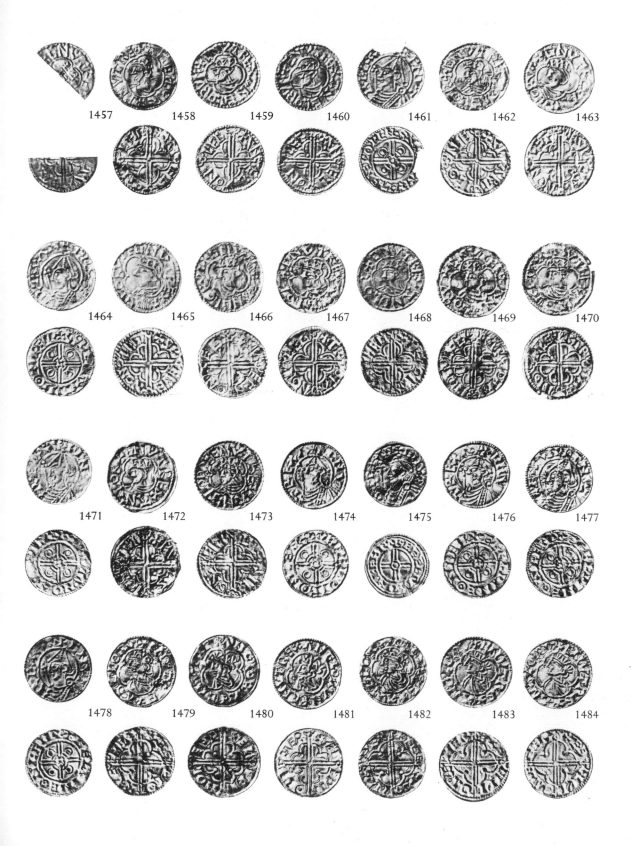

1457   1458   1459   1460   1461   1462   1463

1464   1465   1466   1467   1468   1469   1470

1471   1472   1473   1474   1475   1476   1477

1478   1479   1480   1481   1482   1483   1484

PLATE 54

No.	Weight Gm.	Gr.	Die axis	Moneyer	type	Hild. no.	
LEICESTER (*contd.*)							
1485	1·07	16·5	→	ÆÐELꝦI	E	o	(Rex. on angel.) Overby Lyng find 1865.
1486	1·08	16·6	↓	AÐLꝦI	Eg	1446[1]	Bruun 373. Cracked.
1487							See Canterbury, pl. 6.
1488	1·01	15·6	↗	LOHFM	Ek	1447[1]	Fabricius 1935. Pierced.
1489	1·03	15·9	←	PLACÐEGN	E	o[2]	Bonderup find 1854.
1490	1·14	17·6	↓	PLANCÐEGEN	G	1448	Bonderup find 1854.
1491	1·13	17·4	↓	—	G	1449	Lübeck find 464.
1492	1·09	16·8	←	ꝦVLFNOÐ	E	1450	Gartz, auction 1901, no. 1182.
1493	1·07	16·5	←	—	E	o	Haagerup find 198.
1494	1·05	16·2	↘	ꝦVLNOÐ	E	1455	Bruun 372.
1495	0·80	12·3	↑	—	G	o	Lübeck find 467a.
1496	1·02	15·7	↑	—	G	cf. 1456	Lübeck find 467.
1497	0·88	13·6	←	—	G	1435	Louns find 1870.
1498	0·84	12·9	↓	—	G	1435	Same dies. Bruun 366, ex Bille-Brahe. Cracked.
LIMENA (LYMNE)							
1499	1·00	15·4	↓	GODRIC	G	o[2]	Lübeck find 469.
1500	1·09	16·8	←	—	H	1460	Bruun 377.
1501	1·04	16·1	↑	—	H	1461	Lübeck find 468.
1502	1·09	16·8	↑	—	H	1461	Same dies. Bruun 376.
1503	1·01	15·6	←	LEOꝦINE	E	o[3]	R & D CLXIX. Frost, auction 1827, no. 40.

ADDENDA

1504	(York) see Plate 31.
1505–8	(Hertford) see Plate 44.
230A	(Chichester) see Plate 9.

[1] Scandinavian?—see p. ix.
[2] Moneyer not recorded by Hildebrand for the type.
[3] Moneyer not recorded by Hildebrand for the mint in this reign.

PLATE 54

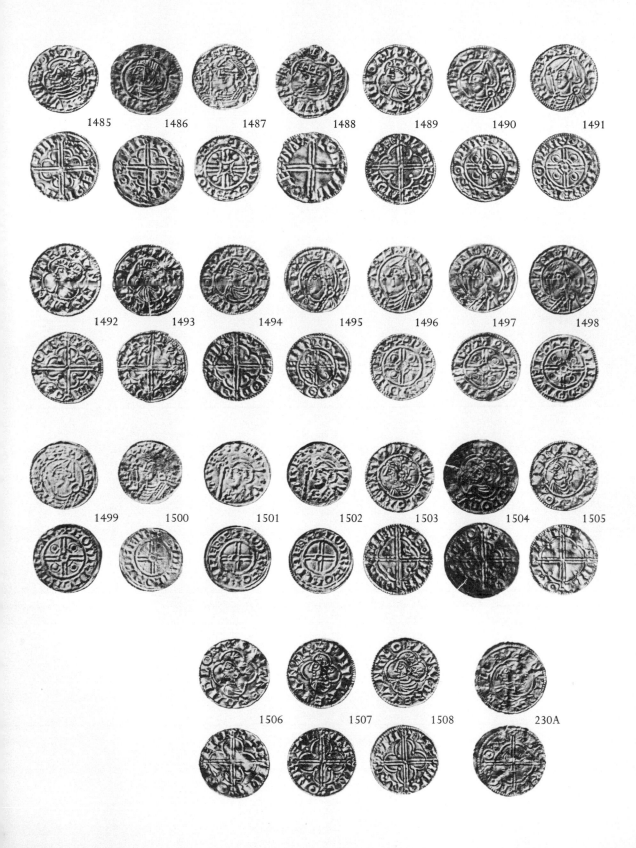

1485   1486   1487   1488   1489   1490   1491

1492   1493   1494   1495   1496   1497   1498

1499   1500   1501   1502   1503   1504   1505

1506   1507   1508   230A